MY MENTAL
MADNESS
MEMOIR

The provocative TRUE journey through my struggles with mental illness

STEPHANIE ANNE ALLEN

Copyright

June 17, 2017

Please Note:

All names, including author's, have been changed to protect their identities.

CONTENTS

My Mental Madness Memoir

The provocative TRUE journey through my struggles with mental illness

By: Stephanie Anne Allen

"Having a mental illness is like a roller coaster ride. You don't jump off while it's still moving. You have to continue to ride, until it comes to a complete stop and you can get off safely."

PREFACE

This book is dedicated to all those individuals inflicted with mental illness, the people in their lives, and to all the mental health care providers that treat them. It is intended not only for entertainment purposes, but for informative ones, as well.

Anyone, who believes and literally can justify in his or her mind that he or she is the next Jesus Christ, is obviously suffering from a major delusion. But probably he or she is having an all-out severe psychotic break. A person having this belief would be defined by ignorant people as being "crazy". But I want to stress, that I do not believe it is appropriate to place labels on the mentally ill, and bring undo judgment upon them. They are people too. They are people who have had to endure intense scrutiny over having such an illness, that is in no way their faults.

That was me. I was the one who believed that I was, what my voices called, "the second-coming of Christ." I thought I was all powerful. I assumed I had psychic and telekinetic powers. My delusional state was even so extreme that I believed I had the authority to end the world, at any time, using my own commands and the power I believed I shared with the Almighty God.

I have schizoaffective disorder—a combination of schizophrenia and bipolar disorder, making it both a thought disorder and a mood disorder. I reasoned in my mind that I was really the new Christ. I was 100% positive of this, after I rationalized all the data. And I was sure that if I denied this identity, that God Himself would strike me dead, and send me to Hell for all of eternity. So, I chose to believe it, even though it was almost impossible for me or anyone else to comprehend.

The world was merciless to my well thought out conceptualizations of the many and varied delusions that I was affected by. The hallucinations, I was also suffering from, only caused me to perceive more validity in my delusions. Despite my persuasive efforts to convince everyone that what I thought was utterly true, they all had other beliefs about what was really going on in my complicated world.

I knew that I had to do something. I had to make some sort of move to escape my personal pain. I concluded that all I could do was embrace my true identity. I couldn't see any other options. I knew that I didn't want to die and go to Hell. I had to accept the fact that God was in control, not me. But it was very difficult to understand how and why God would make me the second-coming of Christ. All I wanted to do was run and hide, but I couldn't, because there is no place you can hide from God.

The delusion that I was Christ was just one of all the many myths that the voices told me were true. God was speaking to me, and I had no doubt in my mind that what I was hearing was indeed, His voice. I also had the ability to speak to live, and even dead, souls. But mostly it was the live souls of the people around me that I communicated with.

Other delusions I had included the beliefs that I had over 500 children, I was the victim of incest, and I was making a movie either for God or Hollywood, to be sold on the internet by imposters. These are just a few of the many diverse delusions that festered deep inside my head. The voices spoke to me constantly, and I was at their mercy. I was so confused and messed up that I felt I had no other choice, but to listen intently to the voices. I came to believe every word they spoke to me. I felt like I was nothing more than a victim of "God's voice." I was hoping He would have pity on me, and release me from the both the pain of my outer world and of my inner world.

I was a dedicated Christian growing up, but now God was telling me that Jesus Christ was "just a beggar they hung to a cross". God also told me that the first Christ did nothing for the world, and I was the one who was going to change the world. I thought I was psychic and telekinetic, and with these powers and God's guidance through His voice, I felt that I could do anything and everything. I assumed that I was invincible and immortal. I concluded, after much justification to myself, that I must surely be God's main servant—the new Christ.

I mean sure God knew who I was, because He created me for this purpose. But I knew that the world would probably not be ready to accept a new Christ. I began to ask myself many questions: Why is God doing this to me? Who am I, after all? Who do the voices say I am?

I feared that convincing the world of my new role would cause me to be locked up in a mental hospital for the rest of my life. Then, if that happened, I worried about how I would be able to save the world, as God had instructed me to do.

So, the question remains: "Am I Christ?"

God spoke this clearly to me, "Yes, you are the second-coming of Christ." His voice was strong and clear. But for some reason, that was hard for me to grasp, because no one could hear God's voice except me. I struggled with taking on this new godly identity. I called myself "God's only daughter". I even believed that my aunt was my true mother and that she was a virgin at the time of conception. It was immaculate conception by an angel. I began to ponder many questions and sought the answers to them.

I prayed and listened closely to God's voice, like I had so many times before. He spoke directly to me, saying, "You are my child. You are the next Christ!" And so, if God is telling me that I am the next Christ, then it must be true. Right? All I really knew was that I loved God and that I had to obey Him, no matter the consequences.

In the back of my mind, I thought that my whole predicament could possibly be caused by mental illness. But I ultimately decided that my reality was too real to be untrue. It had to be true, because I was too strong and too intelligent to have schizophrenia. I thought that only crazy people had that, and I absolutely refused to accept it and be placed in that category. I told myself that this couldn't possibly be a delusion. God really was speaking to me. I was finally "special", and that made me feel good amid my great mental agony.

These insistent voices soon became a constant and harsh reality in my life. They were also of great influence. "It's real. You are the second-coming of Christ," a voice reiterated, repeatedly in my head. This was an extremely vulnerable and lonely time during my life.

I recall, that as a child, I continued to repeat a specific prayer. I asked God to make me a very special and important person. I wanted nothing more than to do something incredible and uncommon with my life. I wanted God and everyone else to be proud of me and have high regards for me. I knew I must strive for perfection, no matter the consequences. This was my chance to prove to God that I was indeed worthy of His love. Also, it was an opportunity for me to gain respect from other people. I would do it. I would be the next Christ, even though I knew this would be a very tough and rocky path to follow. I had to embrace it. I had no choice. It was my destiny, given to me by God Himself.

My illness was so out of control that my life became haywire. My delusional fairyland was extremely rough on me and all the people in my life. I know now that these people only wanted the best for me, but I refused to accept the fact that I indeed was suffering from psychosis. I thought it was easier to come up with bizarre ideas to explain what was really going on in my life. But realizing that you are indeed ill is the first step in recovery. I was not able to admit this to myself. Of course, as you can see, this made it almost impossible for me to get well and obtain any sort of mental stability.

I eventually stopped taking my medication, as the voices convinced me that the medication I was prescribed would kill me. As you can imagine, my life only began to spiral downward at an even faster rate. I continued to believe that I was truly Christ. When taking on such a high status became too hard, I would resort to thinking that I was just the next Job from the Bible. Maybe, my delusions of grandeur just stemmed from the fact that I just wanted so bad to be someone of great importance.

This is the story of my life. It is about a devastating mental illness that causes tragedy, loss, hurt, confusion, and loneliness. But it is also about taking it all in stride, and overcoming great obstacles and barriers. It is the story of a woman who overcomes the odds and goes on to become someone great. It is about both faith in self and in God. This in-depth narrative is not only about how to survive, but also about how to be grateful for the little things in the wake of ultimate defeat. Please take this journey with me into my complicated and confusing life. You will find out if I am truly the second-coming of Christ, or if it is just my subconscious desire, fueled by psychosis, to be someone very special and valuable in this world.

Chapter 1

MY HAPPY CHILDHOOD

March 5, 1979—December 1988

I was born on an unseasonably warm day in the March of 1979. My life began on the fifth of the month at exactly 8:46am. The day of the week I was born was a Monday. I learned from my mother years later, that I was born with my tongue tied down. Apparently, it had not appropriately "split" during my mother's pregnancy. So, the doctors had to cut the tissue under my tongue to rectify the problem. Perhaps this was just the initial sign from God that I should be cautious of speaking before I thought first. I would continue to ponder this notion throughout the length of my life.

My mother was 27 years old and my father was 28, when I arrived in this world. I would join two older brothers, who my parents had named Ronald and Roger. I also had been blessed with an older sister, who was given the name April. As an adult, she would change her name when she was struggling with an identity crisis.

To support the six of us, my hard-working and dedicated father worked long hours at a factory that made cars. At the time, my mom had taken up the daunting and meticulous task of being a dedicated housewife and mother. This was not an easy task, because I don't believe she was really prepared to have three of five children inflicted with mental illnesses. Despite my mother's lack of preparation to take on such a difficult task, she did it with vibrancy and acquired skills.

Until I hit the devastating time of puberty, I was a very happy child. I'll never forget my dad telling me that I was the most "good-natured" of all his five children. I remember how he used to take the whole family on nature trails, and how he would always educate us about all the names and uses of all the plants we would encounter. He also taught us how to survive in the wilderness, in which he had a deep infatuation. In addition, he will be remembered as the "head of the household". My dad made us rubber band guns, taught us how to use tools, and made wooden projects with us. He would take us camping every summer. In addition to all the fun times we spent with him, we also would go on our yearly summer vacation as a family.

He would make tent forts out of blankets for us, and would make snowmen and have snowball fights with us in the wintertime. He was a loving father to all his kids. On some rainy days, when playing softball together in the park behind our house was out of the question, he'd show us old recorded films of ourselves and our other relatives. We would get to see everyone growing old! I recall gathering in the basement and having homemade popcorn that was made by the mom, while watching the projected films. My dad worked afternoons so we rarely saw him on weekdays. Something that really irritated me about him and my brothers was when they would always leave the toilet seat up and not flush the toilet!

I remember that on weekends I'd kiss my dad's cheek and tell him good-night. He'd give me an affectionate kiss right back on my cheek too. He was a proud man who valued his family. He loved all six of us—his five kids (I also have a younger brother named Victor.) and his wife, who was known to me as mom.

Each summer, my mom would plan our vacations. We would travel to many places in Michigan, Ohio, Kentucky, Tennessee, Florida, and even Pennsylvania once or twice. I really enjoyed the amusement parks that we went to. Of course, my favorite rides were roller coasters. I loved the highest and fastest ones the best. A roller coaster ride is much like my life would soon become. But, at the time, I had no clue what life would bestow upon me. I just wanted to be a carefree child.

I remember playing in the bumper cars with my dad, and when I was very young we would hop in a car together. When I got older, I progressed into having my own car. My dad and I would have head on "accidents". It was a lot of fun and brought smiles to my face. I would describe my dad as a fun-loving man. He had wavy black hair and sideburns. Many people often mistook him for an Elvis impersonator. But unlike Mr. Presley, my dad had absolutely no musical ability. He was very smart in his own way though. But most importantly, he loved me, like a father should love his daughter. And I loved him too.

I also loved my mom very much. She was a very committed mother to her children and an excellent wife to my father. As I look at it now, she would absolutely "wait on" all of us and do whatever it took to make us all very happy. She was president of the PTA at my school and was the leader of my Brownie troop and my sister's Girl Scout troop. She was strong-willed and yet loving at the same time.   Her and my father seemed inseparable as they had been high school sweethearts.   My home life was great and comfortable, because I was loved by my entire family, including my mom. She was always there for me and I looked up to her. I would always go grocery shopping with her, and because I helped, she'd always remembered to buy me a little treat as a reward. I enjoyed these trips to the store, because I got to spend one-on-one time with my mom. She used to add things up on a piece of paper to make sure she had enough money to cover the bill.

It's very expensive, as you can imagine, to raise five kids. But we weren't poor. At least I don't think we were. Maybe we were below the poverty level, but my parents never revealed if there was any sort of money problem. My caring mom would always take such good care of me and all my siblings when we were sick. But also when we were well. I recall that she cared so much for me, and I felt truly happy and blessed.

My oldest brother Ronald, who was born just seven months after my parents wed, may have been the initial reason for their marriage. He used to buy special meals for the family. Ronald would earn money from his part time jobs and buy us fast food or pizza delivery. He was a good worker but never did well in school. I remember how generous and kind he was to his siblings, but he also had his flaws. He would spend excessively large amounts of time alone in his bedroom just staring at the ceiling. Ronald was a socially awkward loner, and he really didn't have any friends. At the time, no one really knew he was suffering from a mental illness, probably because of the terrible stigma associated with it. My parents didn't want to believe that mental illness could strike any of their own children. Despite this, my parents did show concern and attempted to get him help through routine therapy and medications.

Roger, my next oldest brother, was blessed by God with the gift of mental stability. He excelled in football at his high school, as a defensive tackle. He also would work out in the school gym, so he could acquire big muscles. I remember that Roger could bench a large amount of weight. He had a lot of friends, too.   But it seemed like he was somewhat of a rebel against my parents, probably just like any normal teenager. I idolized him, and I wanted to be just like him. He became my role model and a hero to me. I even listened to his kind of music—heavy metal. Several times, I hung out with him and his friends.

Roger, who was seven years older than me, had a best friend that was a pervert. One day his so called "friend" took me into the woods and told me to show him my private parts. I refused and ran from the situation.   But because I felt ashamed and embarrassed, I never told a single soul. But I knew that I wasn't going to let this creep ruin a perfectly happy childhood. So, I moved forward with my life like nothing had ever happened.

April, my older and only sister, was born on Christmas Eve in the year 1974. She shared a small bedroom with me, and I always felt like she was trying to take over my space. But in reality, it was me that was invading her area, since she had been born into this world first. She liked to write all kinds of poems and short stories. And the truth be told, April was very good at writing. Perhaps, because of her influence, I also grew fond of writing for a hobby. Looking back, I recall how much she hated wearing dresses, and I can remember her burdensome voice. It was harsh and deep, and it resembled a man's voice rather than a woman's. My parents would always try to get her to dress and act more like a "lady". They were almost to the point of being too extreme with my sister about this issue. I believe this may have been what pushed my sister away and led to her estrangement years later. All my sister wanted to do was be a tomboy, as did I. I feel that my parents may have been too harsh with April simply because of her short hair style and her masculine voice. I looked past those things, and I never judged her. She was my sister and I loved her no matter what. I wouldn't have traded her in for anything or anyone else. I bet being the middle child of five was hard. They say middle children have it the worst. But technically, after my little brother Victor was born, I too could be considered a middle child—being the fourth out of five.

Victor entered this world just seventeen months after I was born. Being very close in age, Victor took the role of being my playmate almost every day. We would ride bikes, play in our sandbox, go to the park, dig up worms for pets, play with our pet salamanders, and climb trees. We did everything together, and we were a constant team. Where you saw one of us, you would always see the other. He was certainly my best friend as a child without a single doubt in my mind. It wasn't all perfect, because we did have our arguments, and we did get in a little trouble together. But, overall, during my years of innocence, I would have to say that he took the title of being my favorite sibling.

I recall that once Victor and I found a purse at the park just setting there and no one was around. We opened it to see who it belonged to, and it was loaded with money in a bank envelope. I wanted to take it to the cops to be returned to the proper owner, because that would be the right thing to do. Victor, on the other hand, wanted to take the cash and dispose of the purse. I won the disagreement, after much discussion. We then took the purse home, and our Aunt Betty called the cops to report that it had been found. Anyways, the owner did end up getting her purse back with all the cash still inside. And it made me feel better than it would have if we would have decided to just keep the money. Returning the purse was the morally right thing to do.

Once, while Victor and I were riding our bikes together, we chose to see what would happen if we rode our bikes head on into each other. I think it may have even been my idea. Well, that obviously didn't go very well for me. I ended up flying over the handlebars and landing head first onto the hard cement sidewalk. I had broken my front tooth, which had been a permanent one. I was taken to the dentist to have it capped. As a child, I felt that was extremely tragic. Guess I had no idea what kind of chaos the rest of life would bring to me.

I recall how Victor and I used to draw and color pictures to sell to nearby neighbors. He was so much better of an artist than me. The neighbors on each side of my parents' house would purchase them from us, but no one else seemed to be interested, for the price of fifty cents each.

As a child, I was enrolled in ballet. I hated it with a deep-seated passion, and I was more than terrible at it. In fact, I was so bad that I was put in a class with all younger girls. They were still better than me! I essentially begged my mother to let me quit ballet. At first, I was trying to make her proud, but after a while, I realized that doing something I sucked at, wouldn't work to make her proud. One day, she finally realized that ballet wasn't "my cup of tea", and disenrolled me. I think she was very happy to save the money that had been involved with the fees. I also bet she realized that I would never be graceful like the other girls. I was just a clumsy tomboy, and that was fine with me.

Growing up, I had a very kind grandmother who lived just two houses away from us, and two dedicated aunts who were often there. My grandma would watch Victor and I frequently. She played cards with us and would purposely cheat, against her own favor, to allow us to win. It wasn't at all uncommon for us to put together these 100-piece puzzles. Sometimes, we'd go over to her house just to hangout and watch one of my Aunt Betty's movies. My aunt had bought many videos, but also had recorded many movies off the television. I recall how my Aunt Betty and my grandma would take us many places, including museums, zoos, parks, beaches, and even a wave pool. They were the two leading adults in my life, and I loved them more than anything. In a way, I thought that they would be in my life forever. As a child, I felt that everyone I loved and cared about would live forever.

Then there was my Aunt Michelle. She was a recovery room nurse at a hospital in Detroit, Michigan. Michelle would tell me many interesting hospital tales. Perhaps, she was a great influence in my desire to become a doctor. Anyways, she looked out after us five kids also, and she was always there if we needed her. Michelle and I didn't always get along. She would always call me "obnoxious". Although Michelle and Betty were sisters, both on my mom's side, they often bickered with each other. They didn't really get along very well, but they did love each other, and I knew that for a fact. Michelle loved baking gingerbread men cookies, and I often helped her make them. My favorite part was decorating them by adding the raisins or currants for the eyes and red hots for buttons and noses. I really enjoyed making the cookies and spending time with her. It was fun and made me feel useful. Besides, I liked accomplishing something. Two other things I recall about Michelle is her taking me to many theatrical performances and also on a road trip.

During my childhood, I found school to be very educating and interesting. I liked learning very much, and it showed in my academic performance. I was an A and B student without even trying. I was well-liked by both my peers and teachers. Although I do remember that when I played, I was told I was too aggressive and competitive. After a while, this would affect my ability to make and keep quality friends.

I walked to and from school every day with my little brother Victor. Once we even saw a dog in someone's yard that looked to me like a bear. I remember screaming "bear", and his immediate response was to protect me. Another time, after walking under a tree on my way to school, a bird went to the bathroom right on the top of my head! White, dirty feces stuck in my long curly red hair.

I was the only redhead in my class, and one, of only a few, in my entire elementary school. Having red hair was probably my first realization that I was different from everyone else, but it wouldn't be my last. I debated whether it was ok or not to be unique. All I knew was that it didn't feel good to be dissimilar. At that time, the nickname my peers had given me was appropriately "Big Red", as I had both red hair and was bigger than all the girls my age.

My family had another nickname for me that was degrading and not at all flattering. They called me "Porky Pig". It was so offending that every time I heard it, my feelings were instantly hurt. This may have led to my very low self-esteem. Victor, whose maturity level was near zero at the time, was the one who expressed that name the most. He seemed to really enjoy teasing me. But the truth was, that at that time, I wasn't even fat. I learned to toughen up and hide my true feelings, despite being an extremely sensitive child. I would become even more sensitive, when I began to transition from childhood into the next phase of my life.

Chapter 2

AN EARLY PUBERTY

January 1989—July 1991

The thing that every child must endure at one time or another, began to happen to me when I was just nine years of age. It was unexpected and undeniably unwanted, but it was inevitable. I was in fourth grade when I started developing. Puberty had hit me. At the time, I felt totally alone and lost. I didn't really have any understanding of what was happening to me. It was quite a very emotional and defining point in my life. I became very subconscious and even more insecure than I already was. All I wanted to do was isolate myself into my own little world and hope that no one was noticing what was happening to me.

I was positive that no girls my age were developing breasts, like I had begun to. My shirts were too tight in the chest area, and I wanted them to be baggy so no one could tell that I was going through puberty. My mother tried to force me to wear a bra, but I at first, I flat out refused. I didn't want to grow up. I wanted to be a child forever. Eventually, I gave in though and wore my first starter bra, which was a hand-me-down from my sister. Sure enough, when my friends saw the bra straps, they made fun of me and mocked me. I was so embarrassed and devastated. All I wanted to do was run and hide. I then made the choice to start isolating myself from my peers. I withdrew from them almost completely and stop playing with anyone during recess. I would just stand by the wall and wallow in self-pity, wondering when the break would be over. I took this time to think a lot about my life.

When I started getting pubic hair, shortly after, I thought I had a disease, but I was too embarrassed to ask anyone about it. I didn't even feel that I could question my mother about what was happening to my body. So, I stayed in the unknown and feared that I had a terminal disease in which I thought I would soon die from. Besides public hair, I began to develop hair under my arms and on my legs. I thought to myself that I was "becoming a hairy mess" but I still didn't want to shave my legs. Once again, I felt forced to comply with my mother's wishes. After all, I had no choice but to grow up. It was bound to happen to everyone except those who died very young. And I didn't want to be one of those who did. Everyone must go through this, I thought. But it was just so new and too hard for me to understand and figure out on my own. I felt so alone, because I didn't feel that there was anyone I could talk to about my concerns.

All I knew in my heart and soul was that I wanted to stay a child forever. I knew I wasn't ready for what was happening to me. I wasn't at all prepared. (My grandmother's motto in life had been "Always be prepared.") Growing up seemed to be so full of responsibilities and that is the last thing I wanted at the tender age of nine. If it would have been possible, I would have avoided the hardships of adulthood by staying a child forever. That is what I wanted—to just be a child forever.

Getting me to use deodorant was yet another battle my mother had with me. Using deodorant is yet another part of growing up, and I wasn't ready to use it because I wasn't ready to grow up. Soon, I realized that I needed it or I would risk smelling bad. So, I began using it, but I was very reluctant to agree. It wasn't until my peers told me I had a body odor that I accepted the fact that I had to use it.

During the summer between fourth and fifth grade, I tried to radically accept the fact that I was indeed becoming a woman, at least physically. Dealing with this mental dilemma led me to live my life as a loner. I continued to isolate myself.   I was terrified of my peers' reactions to my new body. Kids can be so cruel.

During this summer, on August 15th, 1989, to be exact, I started to get unusual pains in my abdomen. I felt a type of pain that I had never endured before. I decided just to relax on the couch. Suddenly, after about an hour or two, the pain came to an abrupt stop. I went to use the bathroom because I felt something wet in my underwear. That is when I saw a few droplets of blood.   I was totally shocked, stunned, and ultimately terrified. I burst into a very agitated crying spell. I told my mother, and she was not sympathetic to any degree. She just reminded me of the "puberty class" that my peers and I had last school year in the fourth grade. It was during that class that all my peers laughed and joked about the subject matter.   No one was taking it seriously. I knew that I surely did not want to be the laughing stock of all my peers by being the first to go through this. Unavoidably, I had started my first period. I was only 10 years old at the time.

It was that same day that I experienced my first bout of dissociative depression. I did not even have a name for it at the time. I felt like I was unreal and that I had escaped into my own little world. This mood that I was in could possibly have been because of hormonal changes and the shock and trauma of beginning my period for the very first time. I was feeling so dark, almost like I was in my own remote universe. It was as if a cloud had distended over my head like a dense fog. I just felt so bad both physically and mentally. I didn't know that this was called depression. Puberty was the start, not only of growing up, but also of my struggle with this eerie and very scary darkness.

Fifth grade began less than a month after I started the predestined fate of all women. I tried to carry a purse with maxi pads in it for when I needed them. But that proved to be unacceptable to me, because everyone wanted to look in my purse, and then I knew they would know my secret. So, I hide the pads in my book bag instead. When it was time to change my pad, I would go to my locker and hide a pad in my pocket. I also would ask to use the bathroom at odd times, so no one else would see me get the pad from my locker or hear me changing my pad.

My periods would stop and go. When I went from sitting or lying to standing, blood would just gush out of me perversely. Blood would get everywhere, and the amount of pain I was in proved nearly unbearable. The blood clots were huge and I thought I was going to bleed to death.

But I never complained about this. I was way too embarrassed to tell anyone for fear of rejection and embarrassment. After all, I was a woman now and I was required to be strong. I fought growing up all I could, maybe I just had to accept it. But the aloneness just continued. None of my peers had their periods yet, so I couldn't understand why I did. I was positive that there was no way I was going to tell them that I had gotten mine for the first time during the summer. It was my deep dark secret, and mine alone.

My fifth-grade teacher put me in "Talent Pool", which is a program for gifted students. So, I guess this proved that I was smart, and my self-esteem increased because of it. I remember how much I enjoyed getting out of regular studies to do some mind empowering activities. Intelligence was the first positive characteristic I ever used to define and describe myself.

During fifth grade recesses, I continued to isolate myself, just like when I had the previous school year. I wouldn't play with the other kids, because I was no longer felt like I was one of them. I was now a woman, while they were still children.

The morning after I started my period, my dad told me that I was "now a woman". I didn't feel that it was the right thing to say. I thought that growing up would cause me to lose the love of my parents, but I ended up being the one that was pushing them away. Here I was between childhood and adulthood, and I had no idea where I fit in.

Soon, I started the sixth grade. This was the last year of elementary school, which caused me to believe that I was growing up after all. It was during this year that I took a fond interest in writing, and I had a talented imagination to work with. I decided I wanted to write for a living. It was a very reasonable goal and I had the motivation and drive to succeed at it, but my mom would always say that no one can make a living as a writer. So, I disregarded my ambition and moved forward to obtain other goals. But I never gave up on my writing. I did it as a hobby. I wrote many poems, stories, and books.

My first book was about two teenagers who were having sex. It started out being a story about an innocent love affair. Then the book became nothing but a provocative story about the sexual acts between this boy and this girl. A male peer requested this, and it was through him that I learned about many of these sexual acts. I wasn't having sex with anyone. They were just telling me all about it. I was letting them read my novel, because I was impressed with my own writing skills and wanted to show off my talent. The book was being passed around for everyone to read. Unfortunately, one of the boys gave it to the teacher, who in turn, passed it on to the principal. I was told that I had done "the most horrible thing in the world", by writing a "porn novel". I wasn't trying to be a bad person. All I wanted to do was prove to everyone that I was growing up because I knew about sex. After that, I vowed to myself and to God that I would not have sex until I was married.

All I knew was that writing made me happy and happiness did not come easily those days. So, I chose to continue to write, but about a different topic. I wrote book after book during the summer between sixth and seventh grade. I didn't do much of anything else, because I was so passionate about my writing endeavors. I was not getting the proper amount of sleep, because of my somewhat obsessive fix on writing. This led to me being diagnosed with mono. Mono is sometimes called "the kissing disease", but I had never kissed, or been kissed by, anyone up to that point in my life.

The mono began to take its toll on my life and caused me to suffer from fevers, chills, and many other symptoms. I slept constantly due to the extreme fatigue I was experiencing. In my mind, I wondered how I could possibly get sick when I had just a month and a half left of summer. I would soon begin middle school, and I knew that I didn't want to miss my first day at that new place.

During this time, my parents started arguing daily. My mother informed me that my father was cashing his work checks and keeping half for himself to use for his obsessive compulsive buying addiction. Also, she told me that he was cheating on her with a woman he worked with. These things caused constant bickering and fights between them. A couple times the cops were called by our neighbors. Home life was beginning to feel like a living hell. I wanted out, and often contemplated running away.

I began to fear for my mother's safety. All I could do was hope my mother would come to her senses and file for divorce. She refused, stating that there were financial concerns. So, my mom decided to stay with him. I guess, even though I was growing up, I was still too young to really understand what was truly going on. This was a very confusing time and many more would follow.

Chapter 3

NOT FITTING IN ANYWHERE

August 1991—August 1993

Just thinking about a new school, with new teachers and the possibility of making new friends, only increased the fatigue I was having. I wasn't going to let this illness stop me from going to my first day of school. I got up early that day, still having a fever and sweats from the mono.

I got on a school bus for the first time in my life, and I was instantly made fun of and teased senselessly by my fellow peers. The bus was packed and there was nowhere to sit. Luckily, a couple of nice girls, whom I knew from my elementary school, scooted over to make room for me. I became the third one on the seat. We hardly fit, and with each turn, I nearly fell off the seat and onto the floor. I hoped that this experience on the bus wasn't going to be a predictor of what would happen when we finally arrived at the school.

When the bus pulled into the school parking lot, I remember my anxiety was at a very high level. I was so nervous and painfully tense. I nearly tripped while exiting the bus, because I was not used to the big steps. I looked around at all these new faces, and all I wanted to do was cry. I felt like I wasn't going to fit in. The entirely new environment, on top of the fact I was suffering from the symptoms of mono, was almost too overwhelming.

I was also still suffering from the mental agony of growing up too early. This caused a festering emotional pain inside me that didn't seem to fade away with time. Now that I was in seventh grade, I thought that some of the girls must have periods by now. I sure wished that I had someone to talk to, someone I could empathize with. All I knew was that I wanted desperately to fit in and have friends again. I craved the social interaction and social acceptance that had been lacking in my life.

At lunch, on that first full day of seventh grade, I didn't know where to sit. I looked around and saw that everyone had their own circle of friends—everyone, but me. Feeling defeated, I took my bagged lunch outside, and I ate it silently and alone under a tree in the schoolyard.

After making it through the seven-class-hour day, I came home by bus with a 102-degree temperature. I would not be able to go back to school until I got over the mono. My mom took very good care of me during this time, but I was still having an extremely hard time kicking the illness in the butt. I was doing all my school work at home and learned on my own through the textbooks. I missed exactly half of seventh grade. Ninety days present and the other ninety absent. But my grades were very good—straight A's to be exact.

Finally, it was time for me to go back to school, because I did eventually get well after months of recuperation. I did go back, but just as I expected, I still didn't fit it.

There was a boy named Jason who wouldn't stop picking on me. His locker was right next to mine due to locker assignments that were based on last names. Jason would say some very awful things to me, and would punch my locker aggressively in a rage. The truth was that I hated him passionately, because he just wouldn't stop harassing me.

Gym class was the worst part of my day. I hated undressing in front of these immature girls. I was a woman and they were just children. To my surprise, some of the girls were developed or at least they had begun the transitional process. I found myself looking at them, almost like some sort of sick attraction that I did not understand at that time. I moved to a locker in a secluded area to avoid myself from feeling this "attraction". I wasn't going to undress in their presence anymore. I was ashamed of my body and of the feelings I was having towards my female peers. I did not understand this "attraction" and was very confused. I knew I was not going to tell another soul about this, because I just felt so ashamed. This was yet another secret I buried deep inside.

During eighth grade, my second and last year of middle school, I noticed that other students were taking advantage of me for being intelligent. I was letting them copy my homework and cheat off my tests. I just wanted to be accepted and liked, and I was going to do whatever it took to achieve that. Despite missing half of seventh grade, I was still a straight A student. Schoolwork wasn't a concern of mine, while having no friends was. I had no one to confide in. I was so lonely. I began to wonder if I'd ever fit in anywhere. I was eating my lunches in the library, isolating myself, because I could hide there and eat in a mindless peace.

The summer between eighth and ninth grade was a summer filled with independent studying. I became really interested in anatomy and physiology. I dissected animals on my own, and read medical books on the human body and about diseases. I even painted models of human organs. I made up my mind, at that point, that I was going to become a doctor. I narrowed it down to just one—an oncologist. I wanted to find the cure for cancer. Before having this ambition in life, I also had dreams of becoming a lawyer, a writer, and a restaurant owner.

I believed that finding the cure for cancer was indeed my sole purpose in this life. Suddenly, I began to believe my life had meaning, even though I was friendless. I would fill the hole inside me from having no friends, with a thriving and successful career. I was motivated, determined, and ambitious. And I would push myself as hard as needed to achieve my career goals.

Chapter 4

THE START OF SEEKING OVERACHIEVEMENT

September 1993—December 1994

When high school started, my main goal in life was to become Valedictorian of my class. I strived hard for complete academic perfection. I thought that perhaps my mother would love me more if I achieved this goal. Maybe she would even be proud of me. I wanted to graduate first, in a class of 267 students, with a perfect 4.0 grade point average. I knew that I must do whatever it took to be successful at this. I studied nonstop. I was very focused, and I put a constant effort into obtaining a successful education. I got A+'s on all my tests and homework assignments. I even got yelled at by my biology teacher, one time, for answering all the correct answers in class!

I continued to have no friends, and an uneasy loneliness continued to stir within my heart. If that wasn't enough, I was becoming manic, although at the time I did not recognize this. I was having racing thoughts and grandiose ideations. It seemed more than just a drive to achieve perfection. This had been the start of my bipolar disorder. At only age 15, I was beginning to be inflicted with the first noticeable signs of mental illness. My mom took me to a local therapist and a psychiatrist, because she was very concerned about my mental well-being.

At therapy, I would sit on the floor and refuse to admit what was bothering me the most—having no friends. Being friendless seemed to me like a totally embarrassing and shameful thing. I felt like a complete failure. I hadn't the faintest idea how to make a friend, and I was too stubborn to admit this to anyone, including my own therapist.

During this disturbing time, I began writing poetry about the darkest things, including my fascination with death. In fact, several were published.

At this gloomy time, I also began my addiction with self-mutilation. I was cutting myself almost daily with rusty razor blades that my dad had just laying around the garage. Slashing myself repeatedly, gave me this rush. I seemed to enjoy the pain and seeing the blood. The blood and the pain were proof that I was a real, true, alive human being. I even carved words into myself. Some of the words I carved were: "lonely", "bad", "suicide", and "crazy". I knew that I was tattooing myself for life with these shameful terms, but I just could not stop. I would cry myself to sleep after I was done. I was so numbed inside. I was mutilating myself to feel real. I even attempted to slit my wrists, but my mom caught me. I was then hospitalized psychiatrically.

My first real experience on a mental ward was one that was filled with extreme chaos and havoc. I was on the pediatric psych ward, because I was under age 18. The patients seemed insane to me and their behaviors were seemingly corrupt and ridiculous. They screamed and carried on, talking about and saying the craziest of things. Some of the patients ran and jumped around 24 hours a day. Others striped off all their clothes during meals. Some even wet and soiled themselves. A few extremely disruptive patients required shots and quiet room visits. They remained in seclusion until they had relaxed. It was very much an insane time. I remember being so scared, because I had the fear that the other patients were going to harm or even kill me. I didn't want to be there, because I felt that I wasn't one of them. I refused to believe that I was crazy just like them. Like everywhere else, I didn't fit in this place. I surely was not going to let anyone call me "crazy" and lock me up in a place like this again.

At the hospital, they discovered I had hypothyroidism, a low functioning thyroid, which can mimic the symptoms of depression. I was prescribed a medication called Synthroid. They also advised me to take Zoloft. This antidepressant was supposed to help with my clinical depression, which they then also diagnosed me with.

Despite the antidepressant medication, the troublesome depression continued to linger. All I knew was that I wanted to die. I wanted to end my life. It became almost like a goal—to commit the final act of suicide. Looking back, I don't really think I wanted to die. What I did want was an end to my pain. I wanted and needed a lot of help. I was totally and completely suicidal. Death seemed like the answer to everything, because I was just so unhappy. I blamed it all on the fact that I had no friends, when in fact, my depression was caused by a chemical imbalance within my brain.

"Why was this happening to me? It just isn't fair," I thought to myself. I was 16 years old and I was full of absolute misery. Most kids, my age, were enjoying life. It just didn't seem right.

I remember, that shortly after my first hospitalization, I argued with a peer who was supporting the gay population. Voicing my

43

family's opinion, I told her how wrong I thought it was to be gay. Upset, she claimed to have put a spell on me for punishment, using witchcraft. Speaking of homosexuals, I had no clue, that I was, in fact, one myself. I was a virgin and I hadn't even kissed a guy much less a girl. I thought I could be gay to some degree, but I was terrified to admit it to myself, much less others. My whole family believed that "all fags, queers, and dykes should be put on an island and shot to death". Therefore, I couldn't let myself accept that I was a lesbian. I had to abide by my parents' rules about life, or ultimately, I would be rejected and disowned by them.

In therapy, I talked constantly about gaining independence from my parents. I wanted to get away from their house to live my own life. I thought that was the secret to happiness. I believed, that after that happened, my depression would just melt away, and I would finally find some happiness in my life. I knew I wanted a relationship. I wanted a companion, a lover, a special friend, and eventually, a soulmate.

I bought my first car from my parents for only $100. It was a brown 1986 Ford Aerostar. A few months later, after a very stressful therapy appointment, I rear-ended someone and totaled it. Using the money, I had saved up from working, I was able to purchase another car. I loved driving, because it gave me a sense of freedom and control. Both of which, I felt that I was lacking in my life.

During this time, age 16, my faith really began to shatter and fall apart. I wondered why God was letting me suffer so much. I felt like God was punishing me, for some reason, by inflicting all this sorrow into my life. I began to relate to the story of Job from the Bible. I was raised Catholic, but I was unable to relate to the Church services that my parents took me to every Sunday. Also, Bible school on Saturdays did not seem to help. It was very strange that I was told by a priest that I should become a nun! I knew in my heart that I was not meant to be a nun. I believed God had very special plans for me. I was sure of it. I had to maintain some hope in my life. But despite this little spark of hope, I began to doubt God and everything that He was all about.

Sometimes mania felt good to me. I would feel so high without even using illegal drugs. But it was dangerous also because it led me to do impulsive and scary things. Not only was I suffering from many bouts of hypomania, I was having full blown episodes of mania. Sometimes it felt like such a rush with all the extra energy and euphoria involved.

Depression, on the other hand, was hard, difficult, dark, and lonely. I remember how lonely and empty I felt on the inside. All I wanted to do was sleep and cry constantly. When the pain became too much, I would resort to my dysfunctional coping skill of cutting myself. This seemed to be the only way, other than suicide, to release my hidden agony.

At the time, I even had three jobs, all while attending high school full time as a straight A student. I felt like a "super human". I felt like I could achieve anything and everything. All I needed to do was push myself as hard as possible, and this was exactly what I did.

I had guinea pigs for pets, who brought much comfort to my out-of-control life. When I talked to them, they never judged me or made fun of me. I loved them so very much and they loved me too. They were my only friends. During the summer, I would take them out on the lawn and let them enjoy the sunshine, while they feasted on grass. I had this deep connection with them that I was unable to find with any human being. They were the support that I leaned on while I worked towards accomplishing my almost impossible goals.

Chapter 5

ACCOMPLISHING A HUGE GOAL

January 1995—June 1997

During the second semester of my sophomore year, I was so extremely depressed that I stopped studying almost completely and wanted to give up my goal of becoming Valedictorian. Despite this, the A's kept coming to me. I knew God must be on my side and that with His help, I would still be able to graduate first in my class regardless of my infliction with mental illness. I wanted that more than I wanted to die. I had worked so hard my first three semesters in high school and I had a very hard life, so I felt like I deserved this. I tried to concentrate on my studies, but concentration was very difficult to maintain, because of my mental instability.

Therapy continued and so did the medication regimen. The psychiatrists tried nearly every medication that was available on me to see what worked best to control my symptoms. They also diagnosed me with Borderline Personality Disorder during this time. My trouble with interpersonal relationships was among many of the tell-tale signs.

I learned to balance school and work. But I continued to have no social life. I wanted friends so bad, and I knew I had to do something about that. So, I decided to join the marching band. I knew nothing about music, musical instruments, or the physical agility it would take to march. I decided to play the trumpet but was given a coronet to play instead. During the summer between my junior and senior years, I studied music, but was unable to acquire any musical skills. I had no ear for music, and besides that, I was totally tone deaf. I did manage to get the marching part down, which impressed the teacher. I even got an A in the class for the high level of effort that I had displayed. Despite my suicidal tendencies, I liked band camp, at least a little. The musical performance that we put on was very motivational. Still, I had no idea how to make friends.

Finally, it was time to graduate. I had made my dream come true. I would go forward as first in my class, but there was a major problem. Six other fellow students would be Valedictorians as well. I was upset, because I wanted to have this title for my very own. I wanted to be the lone Valedictorian of the class of 1997. I wanted my mother to be proud of me. I did not think she would be as proud of me if I had to share the title, and especially with six others!

Just a month before the graduation ceremony, I attempted suicide by overdosing on prescription pain killers. I couldn't deal with my life anymore. It just seemed so impossible. After two long weeks in the mental hospital, for the second time, I was released. I had to write my speech for graduation, and I only had two weeks to do it. I had been putting it off, fearing I would not be able to make it "perfect". I thought perfection would make me special and get me friends. All I knew was that I wanted my speech to be a complete success. I sat down at my desk and began to think, and finally I had what seemed like the perfect idea. I would write my speech about unconditional love. I began to write, and at the time, I thought the vernacular would be a victory for me. The actual speech is below.

"We are gathered here today to celebrate the joyous occasion of graduation. I stand here tonight representing each and every one of you. Everyone should have a dream. Today my dream is coming true. For the last four years I have worked for this, and now I would like to share with you the most important lesson of life. And that is to appreciate life itself. Love with all your heart. Find happiness in yourself, no matter what

49

problems and hardships life may throw at you. You can overcome them.

Believe me I know.   And now that I am happy again, I love each moment of my life.   I love the trees, the birds, my health, my family, my friends, but most importantly myself.   I thank God, each day that I have these things. Because if we lose everything and everyone, including our own life, then we would have nothing.   Each thing or person you have in your life is merely there to enrich your life.   The person who will be with you for the rest of your life is you.   Love yourself, because until you do, you will never be able to love another.   Love your family, friends, neighbors, and even each tiny blade of grass. The greatest gifts of all are love and happiness. Without these you would be unable to enjoy life's simple pleasures.

Everything and everyone has a purpose. We are meant to be on this Earth. Be happy with knowing that you are a unique and special person with a place in the world.   Because you never know when it may all be taken away from you. But rejoice in the fact that it is all part of a larger plan.

No matter how hard life may seem you can get through it.   Your future will be bright. You can be whoever you want to be.   You can do whatever you want to do. You are free to explore the world.   But always remember to love everything and everyone, to be happy, and to always have a dream.

I would like to thank my family and my friends, who have helped me achieve my dream of today and will help me strive for success in the future. I love all of you.   I wish for the class of 1997 a bright and beautiful future."

As you can see from this original version on my Valedictorian speech on graduation day, I was a very messed up individual because despite my message of dreams, love, and happiness, I had none of those things. I was a hypocrite. But inside there must have been some degree of hope. After all, hope is all I could have at that moment in time. I wanted to have love, and I longed to be happy. As for my dreams, that's another story. Sure, I had dreams, but I feared I would not be able to accomplish them due to the severity of my mental illness. But I was right to worry about that, because my mental illness surely would get in my way of my goal of becoming a doctor. Perhaps God had a very different life for me than the one I wanted for myself. I would try to embrace God's plan.

During the writing of this speech, I was concerned it was no good. So, I wrote and ripped it up, time after time. I couldn't concentrate on anything, especially writing something perfect to make my parents proud. During the process, I drove to a fast food restaurant for a break. I thought I might be able to concentrate better there. I ordered some lunch and attempted to guide my hand across the paper with a pen. Maybe I should take notes first or do an outline, I thought. Ok. Here goes. I'll write about family and friends. But I don't have any friends, I remembered. Then a very nagging and anxious feeling came on. I wondered if I was going to continue to be lonely when I went to college in the fall. Things were changing. I was changing. Heck, I didn't know what to write my speech about. I had two hours left to complete the dialogue. So, I recall, I just wrote what was in my heart, until it was completed. I felt it was a masterpiece.

Now that it had been written, my focus was on how to present this to thousands of people. I had to make myself ready. I remember thinking that it was supposed to be the happiest moment in my life. I had done it. I had accomplished my first huge goal.

I stood there, knees shaking, and gave my speech. But nothing happened. It wasn't like I had pictured it would be. I didn't feel the happiness I thought I should have felt. As a matter of fact, I felt nothing, but my unending depression. I had become Valedictorian, but I just didn't care anymore. I wasn't ecstatically happy, like I imagined I would be. In fact, I felt absolutely no happiness whatsoever.

Death was still on my mind, despite achieving my goal. I kept thinking I should kill myself and be with my guinea pig, who had died just a few months prior. I had lost my best friend. I thought that maybe I should go and be with him. He was my rock, and truthfully, he had been my one and only unconditional friend.

I could only wonder what would happen next to me in this life. . .

Chapter 6

BIG CHANGES AHEAD

June 1997—September 1997

The summer between my senior year of high school and my freshman year of college was a period of big changes. I had to grow up fast, by choosing to be a responsible adult over being an immature child. I tried, but my mental illness was still gripping a very strong hold on me. I had super highs and super lows. The depression, which was more common for me, hung on like a dark cloud over my head. My death seemed inevitable. I knew I was going to die sometime, but I wanted to hurry up the process. I was suicidal constantly with intense feelings of worthlessness, hopelessness, and helplessness.

At my graduation party, I had some uninvited guests. They were younger than me, and they were gothic. Eager to make any friend that I could, I introduced myself. To my surprise, it was easy to befriend them. My mother called them "freaks", and she highly disapproved of them. But despite this, I spent my whole summer hanging out with them, even though they weren't very good friends at all. They smoked, drank, and did pot. They even beat me up once and stole my

ATM card. When I realized they had stolen it and were using it, I took my parents' advice and called the cops. In the end, I realized that they were just using me for money and rides. I was devastated, and I began to again wonder if I would ever have any "true" friends.

The "freaks" caused me to total my second car. They were smoking pot in the backseat and acting totally crazy. This distracted me from driving properly. I admit that I did try a joint once, but I hated the way it made me feel and plus it was illegal. So, I decided I didn't care to make a habit out of it. Instead, I took up the bad habit of smoking cigarettes on a regular basis.

When I had the "freaks" as friends, I did all the giving. They did all the taking. This would soon become a common theme in all my future relationships. It didn't seem fair. All I wanted was real and true friends, not just someone to hang out with and be used by. I wanted someone to talk to who wasn't going to take advantage of me. I longed for someone to share unconditional love with. I needed someone to love and be loved by.

During this summer, I experienced my first kiss from a man. I felt absolutely nothing for him and did not enjoy it at all. For some reason, I did not find any man to be attractive. I was very pensive. I thought that I might be gay, but because of my upbringing, I felt forced to believe that this was wrong and immoral. So, I chose to harbor this nagging feeling deep inside and not think about it. I was straight. I had no choice. That was the end of it.

I was excited to have a new start when I went away to college. I planned on making lots of friends. I wanted to be popular for a change. While I waited for the semester to start, I read self-help books on how to make and keep friends. I was preparing myself for what I sincerely hoped would be a good year. I knew I wasn't going to be a straight A student, because unlike high school, now was my time to shine socially. Good grades hadn't made me happy, but I believed that finding good and loyal friends would. I felt in my heart that I deserved friends, and I prayed for that. I hoped that God would hear my prayers, but was experiencing major doubts that He even existed.

....

That's the ending of my childhood years. They were filled with problems, chaos, mental illness, and friendless times. I learned that perfectionism was not the answer. I knew the answer was love, and that was what I was longing for so badly. I hoped that college would change me from an insecure little girl into a confident woman. I had to prepare myself. I knew I could no longer rely on my parents for everything. I had to embrace independence and responsibility. This scared the crap out of me.   I feared that the difficult times would continue when I went away to college. I thought I would be all alone without any support system in place. I was afraid that I would have severe difficulty making friends, like I had in the past. As the summer ended, I packed my bags and got ready to leave, almost to the point of being reluctant. This was just another chapter in my life that had ended. Soon, I knew, another door would surely open.

Chapter 7

COLLEGE LIFE AND SEXUAL EXPERIMENTATION

September 1997—May 1998

I knew, almost instantly, that we were not going to get along. While she was outspoken and loud, I was very quiet and reserved. She would bring her boyfriend over to spend the night, which I did not like or agree with. I would have hated having any roommate, but I especially hated having one like her. She must have disliked me too, because she chose to move out. I was left all alone in my dorm room and it became even easier to isolate myself.

I would cut class almost daily, but I continued to maintain a B grade-point-average. I would cry constantly, because I was so damn depressed. I could hardly get myself out of bed most days. When I did get out of bed, it was to eat. I would eat uncontrollably huge amounts of unhealthy food. That led me to get fat. I gained 30 pounds that single school year that I was living on the college campus. Food had become one of the only sources of comfort that I felt I had. The other was tobacco and I had already begun smoking a pack every day. I spent most of my time crying frantically. I managed to make a few friends at first, but lost them quickly due to my big opinionated mouth. I finally gave up trying to make and keep friends. I decided, stubbornly, that I didn't need anyone in my life.

Feeling hopeless, I resorted to never leaving my dorm room. I cut myself violently with razor blades, sometimes using random slashes, but also carving degrading words into my own skin. Hundreds of scars remain as a bitter reminder of those days. Days in which I was completely and utterly miserable. Days where I missed my mom and longed for the comforts of home. My depression had hit an all-time high, and because of this, I was not able to function properly and lead a normal life.

During this awful and depressingly dark time, I willfully experimented with alcohol. I got drunk a few times, but concluded that drinking was not for me. I honestly hated the taste and disliked the rollercoaster ride that it put me on. This rollercoaster ride could be avoided by not drinking, but the bipolar disorder that I suffered with, put me on a whole different and more confusing ride.

I wanted to be social, and I wanted friends desperately. So, I decided I would attempt to start a group for fellow students with depression. Despite my efforts and high hopes, it was a failure, like so much else in my life. I got even more depressed and continued to think of myself as a loser, a failure, and as someone who would always be friendless.

I knew I had to come up with a new and better idea at this very difficult point in my life. I thought that I could possibly get friends by sexually pleasing people. Sure, it wasn't a moral and ethical idea, but I would do anything to make friends. I met a few men who attended the same college on a local chat site. I invited them over to my dorm room and gave them oral sex. I had no idea how to even do it. I found the act totally disgusting, but I was desperate to make friends and I thought that this was the only way. One guy brought me alcohol in exchange for this sexual pleasure. I learned very quickly that these men were not really my friends. Two men tried to have actual intercourse with me, but I didn't want that. I was a virgin and I wanted it to stay that way.

One day, out of the blue, I decided it was the right time to lose my virginity. After all, I was almost 19 years old and this was something that I believed all grown-ups did. I wanted to try it and push my way into adulthood. So, in February 1998, I decided that I would try sexual intercourse for the first time. It lasted for not longer than a minute. I remember how I absolutely hated it. I felt that the act was very degrading and disgusting, without the guy calling me fat and walking out on me, in addition. I then realized that I had done the wrong thing. I knew I should have waited. Perhaps, I should have waited until I was married. I just wasn't ready for sex. I wasn't in love. In fact, I barely knew the guy. I think his name might have been Paul, but to tell you the truth, I don't even remember. Another insistent problem was that I did not find any man to be attractive.

I believed that if men wouldn't like me, maybe women would. There are some lesbians out there, but I didn't know where to find any of them. I thought that maybe I should try the "other side" just to see if I was indeed a homosexual. After all, I had a deep desire to be loved. And whether I wanted to admit it or not, I found women to be very attractive. So, I looked on the internet to find a lesbian, and I managed to find someone within just one week of beginning my search.

Emily was from Pennsylvania and was a freshman in college also. She had never been with a woman either, but she expressed to me that she wanted to try it. So, after talking on the phone for about a week and hitting it off, we decided to meet and make this lesbian thing official. I made the long drive, of nearly nine hours, to her parents' house in Pennsylvania. I stayed there for a total of 4 days. After kissing her for the first time, I became standoffish and almost scared of how intense it was. I began to question the morale of this homosexual act. But within just a few seconds, I had made the decision to continue with this sexual affair. Besides it felt very, very good. And so, we had sex repeatedly during my stay there.

I began confusing sex with love. I thought I had fallen in love with her. Unfortunately, she had not fallen in love with me. I had just been a sexual experiment. But it was fun and exciting. It was a major marker in my life, because now I knew. I knew I was a lesbian. Now, I had to make the very painful journey to cope with and accept that. I knew how my parents and my entire family felt about homosexuality, and I knew that it wasn't going to be easy by any means.

When I left Pennsylvania, I had countless tears flowing from my eyes. I didn't want to leave Emily, because I feared that I would never see her again if my parents found out. I felt a deep connection with her. Emily had been my first woman and she would always hold a special place within my heart.

After nearly getting kicked out of school my freshman year for self-mutilation, the summer had finally arrived. I wanted to see my PA crush again, so I told my mom I was taking a trip to Pennsylvania. Then, I impulsively made the decision to come out with the truth. I told my mom that I was in love with a woman. She started screaming hateful and horrible things at me. She wouldn't back down with her irrational opinions. She refused to let me see my female crush ever again. I was staying with my parents, and they had strict rules that I was obligated to follow. Their rule was that their children shall not be "fags". Inside my heart I felt a deep hole, an eerie emptiness. My first love was gone. I felt so horrible that I started burning myself with cigarettes on my left forearm. I was hurt, ashamed, and alone, because I had been banned from even calling her on the phone. I wasn't even given the opportunity to say goodbye.

Being torn apart from Emily could never stop the memories from that sexual encounter. Kissing her, my first female kiss, was like kissing heaven. I felt like I was in Heaven, or something like that. The truth is that I don't even remember if I had an orgasm or not, but I do remember how intimate we were. Up to that point in my life, she was the person I had felt closest to. I wanted to be with her more than anything. Years later, I disappointingly found out that after she tried another female sexual encounter with someone else, she made the decision that she "didn't want to be gay". Her excuses were that she was a Christian and she wanted children.

I began to question if being a lesbian was against God. After all, it was in the Bible. I eventually concluded that the Bible was written by man and man is bias. Surely, God loves and accepts all His people, even the gay ones. I desperately wanted God to be on my side. I had even attended several church services while I was away at college.

My sister and I had gone to the same college. I had been a freshman, while she was a senior. I would occasionally hang out with her, but she was preoccupied with her own journey of self-discovery. At that time, there was no indication that April was struggling with her sexual orientation and a secret desire to transition into a man. She wrestled with her demons, but she had friends to lean on, unlike me. I was alone. Even though I had my sister, I didn't feel I could share my secrets with her. I feared that she would tell my mother, who I thought would then reject me. Inside, I continued to long for my mom's unconditional acceptance and love, of the real me.

And so, after nearly getting kicked out of school for self-harm, my freshman year of college came to an end. It was finally over. Now I had to start thinking about what I was going to do next with my life.

Chapter 8

LOSING MY SISTER

May 1998—September 1998

Losing my sister, April, was very difficult for me, because not only had I lost her physical presence in my life, but also because she had officially decided to make her break in this world as a lesbian. This made me feel almost envious of her. While she had obtained freedom, I, on the other hand, was still caught in an emotional bondage because of my parents' morals.

April had never completed college like she had planned. Her schizoaffective disorder had ruined her plans for her future. Her illness was unknown to anyone who knew her, and even to herself. I mean our family did notice some depressive symptoms in her, but no one had ever expected that she was dealing with such a very serious and chronic mental illness. Due to her constant mental struggles, she began flunking out of her classes. My sister also was contending with her sexual orientation, like I was. It made me wonder how both my parents' daughters could be gay. Was it nature or nurture? All I knew was that we needed our mother's love and acceptance of our true selves. I began to wonder if we even truly deserved this.

April, who was four years my elder, had met a woman named Linda at college earlier that year. She thought she had fallen in love with this woman, whom she now describes as being "controlling and manipulative". But at the time, she had not seen or even sensed this. Due to my family's bias, she saw only one option for herself and her future with this woman. She made the decision to move to California and start a new life. She had to get away from the conservative nature of the life she had known. She sold all her property, so she could afford two one-way bus tickets to San Francisco.

After April and her lover arrived in the new city, they were penniless and were forced to secure lives as homeless individuals. Linda broke up with April, shortly after arriving in the new place that they would call home. She was so upset that she tried to kill herself by taking a whole bottle of aspirin. This is when she was admitted into the mental health system in California.

My mother was very distraught to learn that her oldest daughter had departed from her life to begin her livelihood somewhere new. Truly, what had bothered my mother most was the homosexual lifestyle that April had chosen to partake in. My mom had the preconception that California was "the land of the fruit and nuts". To put it lightly, she was very prejudice and judgmental. She was someone who was also very stubborn to the idea of change.

I loved my sister and wanted her to come home. I missed her so much. Besides, I felt like we now had a lot to talk about regarding our lifestyles. April refused to return home because my parents were always trying to change her. They weren't ready to accept having a homosexual daughter and now they had two. I had felt obligated to lie to my parents by telling them that I was now straight. I wanted to maintain some level of harmony among us. April, unlike me, dressed in male clothing, which led my mother to constantly harass her.

I knew that my sister was alive and breathing, but now she was thousands of miles away. It just felt like I had lost my sister to an unexpected death. Losing my sister proved to be a very traumatic experience for me. A very deep, hidden hurt was within my heart. It showed in the way I presented myself. I had begun to withdraw and isolate myself even more than I had done previously. I felt perplexed without her.

I started to ponder my life and the opportunities that I was giving up by remaining in the lie of my current "straight as an arrow" lifestyle. I felt that I would be alone and lonely forever. I thought that maybe I should run away too. This would bring me freedom and I could be reunited with my sister. I seriously considered leaving. By staying where I was, I felt that I was giving up my right to be who I really was. Maybe I didn't even truly know who I was, but I did know that I was a lesbian.

I felt that my family would never love and accept me. They would never be able to maintain any amount of unconditional love for me if I veered from the straight life. I really didn't know what to do at this point. I did know however, that I would always stay in touch with my sister. I also knew that she probably had many of the same feelings that I had, including those of confusion, loss, emptiness, and loneliness. Someday I knew that her and I would be reunited, once again. We would be one happy family and best friends. But for now, I would need to move forward without her presence and spirit in my life.

Chapter 9

ACCEPTING DEFEAT

September 1998—May 2002

My sophomore year of college was spent commuting to and from a community college, while holding a job part-time. I was no longer capable of attending a full-fledged university, where I would have to live alone with no support. My parents worried about my safety, especially while I had been away at college, because I was constantly engaging in self-mutilation and had very strong suicidal tendencies. I needed their support, because I was dealing with a very serious and destructive mental illness. It seemed that everyone else in my life had just discarded me when I needed them most, but my parents were always there for me. I now believe that they are the reason that I sustained my very existence during that time.

So, I moved back home officially and accepted my reduced status of being a community college student. Home life was good, but only if I maintained my fronted status of being straight. My mother would read my textbooks to me, because I was unable to concentrate and comprehend them due to my mental decline.

My studies were strained and my grades reflected this. Once a straight A student in high school, I now had a B- average. I tried as hard as I could in college, but every effort seemed exhausting and unproductive. I was too sick to obtain any better grades than I was. My Aunt Betty also read my school books to me, and she corrected all my spelling and grammatical errors on my papers and homework.

I felt I had done the best I could during college with all that life had given me. I recall receiving the letter grade of a D in two classes, political science and sociology. I was forced to take them over for a second time. After retaking the political science class and getting a C, I received my Associates Degree in Science. After repeating the sociology class, I got the credit I needed to continue my education and get a Bachelor of Arts Degree. I even had the unrealistic goals of obtaining a Master's Degree and then a Doctorate.

I decided that becoming a medical doctor would be impossible for me to achieve because of the severity of my mental illness. I knew I had to radically accepted this and chose to move forward with my life in a different direction. My decision to change my major from pre-med to clinical psychology was not an easy one, because it seemed like I was giving up on all my dreams. There was nothing else I could do. I felt that I was incapable of becoming any kind of doctor, and this made me feel like I was a major failure, a loser, someone who was unable to achieve any amount of success. I could only wonder what would happen next.

My mind became preoccupied with all the many questions that were perinate in my life. I began to question why I even existed. I wondered what my purpose was. I deliberated if I would ever be happy. Certain themes always popped up in my head: death, darkness, despair, agony, and loneliness. I constantly thought that the only solution for terminating my mental torture was to end it all. The answer I believed was suicide, but I was too weak. Although I felt that it might have been the only answer, I was too afraid of the finality of death.

During this time, I totaled three more cars. Once, it was because, I fell asleep at the wheel due to the side effects of the Depakote I was prescribed for my then bipolar diagnosis. I was suffering from severe exhaustion. I drove my car right off the road and straight into two mailboxes. When it happened, I went into complete shock. Despite the cracked windshield and blown tire, I drove the rest of the way to school. Later, after speaking with my mom about the incident, I returned to the site of the accident. I admitted to the people that I was at fault for destroying their mailboxes. They ended up being very nice people and they did not call the police to file a report. Luckily, I had missed a cop's mailbox, before I went on to hit the next two mailboxes, one of which belonged to a preacher.

There was another time when I rear-ended someone on the expressway, and then the time I rear-ended a street sweeper. That accident happened because it was causing a widespread haze of dirt and there was absolutely zero visibility. After hitting the street sweeper, another truck rear-ended me. I had been sandwiched in. For this mishap, I received my fourth accident ticket. By age 23, I had only received one speeding ticket but four tickets for car accidents. I was on my fifth car by that age. I could purchase each car with no financial help because of my employment status and savings.

I always had a job but work was very eradicated. I got fired from a McDonalds job, that I had for years, for throwing a piece of cheese at a fellow employee who had thrown a pickle at me. I moved to acquire a new job at a different McDonalds. I got fired from there after they found out that I had been hospitalized for psychiatric reasons. They were unable to accept the fact that I had a mental illness.

So, then I tried working at a retail store, in which I was terminated after three days, for writing "I love you" on a fellow employee's orientation booklet. I then tried working in a group home for the developmentally disabled, as a direct care worker. I was forced to quit there because I was unable to work the late hours. My sleep cycle was getting really screwed up and this was severely impacting my already frail mental state. I even got fired from my internship at the Red Cross for telling all my horrible secrets about my mental illness to a peer. Then I got fired from another fast food job that I was only at for a few months. Again, it was for the reason of being psychiatrically hospitalized, for the fifth time in my life, and the employer's intolerance of this.

I then moved on to a job at a drug store. In a year, I was promoted to the position of key manager. It was during this job that I met a customer named Joshua who showed interest in me. He gave me a greeting card with his phone number in it. He was a sweet and very innocent guy. I thought that I might give him a chance, because I believed it would please my parents. But deep down, I knew I was really gay.

During these few years, I had ballooned up to a weight of 330 lbs. I ate to release my emotional sorrows. I ate when I was really sad, really happy, really confused, really disheartened, really bored, really whatever. The extremeness and intensity of each emotion led to the degree that I would consume food. If something caused me to feel an extreme feeling, I ate, because I felt that eating helped to level out the intensity of each emotion I was experiencing. The feelings of loneliness and emptiness were the main culprits that led to my fascination with food. Dang it anyways, food tasted good, especially fast food, fried food, and sugary food.

I felt that I needed to reward myself for living such an impossible life. I didn't know of any better reward than food. I had lost interest in all other things, because of my illness. In addition to calming my shifts in emotions, eating for me was also a reward for staying alive and not taking my own life.

Between work, school, and my struggle with mental illness, I was incredibly stressed out and overwhelmed. I felt that I just had too much to deal with. I was now in therapy full time, going sometimes twice a week. But I never admitted my true feelings about the loneliness I felt. I was just too embarrassed and too ashamed to admit to my therapist, or anyone, for that matter, that I had no friends. So, I lied to her by making up stories about friends that didn't truly exist. I sat on the floor in the therapy room, dressed in all black, and never really said much at all. But I did share some of my "death poetry", which was later published, with this older lady who never comprehended a word of it.

The therapy experience, at least with my first and longest running therapist, was not very beneficial to me at that time. I tried to tell her my longing for a relationship with a woman, but I was unable to connect with her on any level. I felt that she wouldn't understand me anyways. I felt that no one would ever be able to grasp the amount of emotional pain that I was dealing with.

In addition to the therapy I was receiving, I was on routine psych medications. These meds were changed repeatedly, as they were found to be ineffective even in the higher dosages. Many different medications where analyzed in my treatment to obtain the most effective drug therapy. After some years, it was determined that the best antidepressant for me was Zoloft and the best mood stabilizer was Lithium. At that time, I was not taking an antipsychotic medication because I hadn't yet been diagnosed with a thought disorder.

My official diagnosis at that time was Bipolar Disorder type II. But despite not yet being given the diagnosis of schizoaffective disorder, this is the time I began to have my first psychotic symptoms. No, nothing severe yet, but that was not to say the signs wouldn't become severe. In fact, my psychosis would cause terrible things to occur in my life. But that was yet to come.

My first symptoms of psychosis may have started as a child, but I was not able to recognize it then and neither was anyone else. I was just described as a "very imaginative child". I had a life-size doll and once I believed that I saw that doll move its head and arms. Yes, this lifeless bag of cloth was shifting about. I was sure of it. I remember how scary it was to me at the time. I was about nine years old. Another psychotic event occurred years later, when I envisioned a toy top spinning by using my mind to cause the motion.

One of my most memorable hallucinations occurred when I was in a psych hospital for depression at about 18 or 19 years old. I woke up with pain in my back, like someone had cut into the skin near my right shoulder blade. It was a stabbing pain. I remember looking in the mirror at my back, and sure enough I saw stitches! A huge delusion, which transpired from that hallucination, was that someone had implanted a device in my back. I was certain of it. I concluded that it was a "radio transmitter", and the government was spying on me through this device. I believed their motive was to rid the world of homosexuals. I believed that the government was trying to study me because I was a lesbian. This experience was very bloodcurdling. I was frightened beyond belief.

I kept on pondering why the government would want to do this to me. I might be gay, but I was an extremely kind person. I did many good things for others, including complete strangers. I would help anyone who needed a hand. And now, I believed that the government was listening in on all my conversations and could hear every sound I made. They were snooping in on my business through this radio transmitter that they had implanted in my back!

During this same hospitalization, I believed they had secretly installed a camera in my shower and were watching me take showers. I was extremely embarrassed to be on camera naked. I remember there being a little hole in the ceiling of the shower room, which I believed they were spying on me through. I stuffed it up with toilet paper every time I took a shower. I felt so ashamed by the whole situation. I just couldn't understand why these doctors, who were supposed to be professionals, were doing this to me. All I knew was that they were. And I hated it with a passion.

During my next psych hospitalization, I remember that I had this delusion that my own mother had sold my eggs to a gynecologist so that other women could purchase them. At age 17, I had to have surgery to "fry" my uterine nerves because of the severe pain I was having during my periods. And this, I alleged, was the time that my doctor and my mother had come to this corrupt and illegal agreement. I believed that he had given her thousands of dollars, which motivated her to do it. The doctor's motive was simply greed. He could make an enormous amount of money by selling my eggs. I believed that everyone wanted a smart redheaded child. This delusion only intensified when I began to believe that I had biological children out there who were being created with these stolen eggs. I did not know how many, but I knew that as time elapsed, I would have many more additional children as each egg was used. I hated my mother for doing this to her own child simply for the sake of pure and utter greed. I mean I had children and I had never even been pregnant. All I knew was that I really wanted to get to know each one of them.

During this hospitalization and future ones, the doctors, nurses, and even other patients toiled with me and played with my already weak mental state. They thought I was funny, and made me into some sort of big joke. A few of the patients claimed that they were making a movie about me. This deeply affected me by causing many of my future delusions. I remember running frantically around the hospital ward, in front of the security cameras, and speaking to the cameras as if I was making a movie.

I also recall screaming insane things randomly and making outlandish allegations. I thought the doctors were going to kill me because I was gay. The psychiatrists, who saw that I was suffering, placed me on an antipsychotic. I cannot recall which one, but it must have worked because soon after taking the medication, the psychosis seemed to "wear off". It had begun to gradually dissipate. When I became stabilized, I was released from the hospital.

College life ended on May 5th, 2002, when I graduated with a BA in clinical psychology. Unlike high school, I wasn't even an honor student, but I had undeniably made it. I was really, finally, going to graduate and move on to the next chapter of my life. I began wondering what I should do next with my life. Should I be a case manager or should I continue my schooling and become a therapist? I had to radically accept that I couldn't complete any more schooling. I had struggled so hard just getting a Bachelors, due to my declining mental state. I determined that I would try to find a job as a case manager. My dreams of becoming a doctor were already over. Now I had to give up my alternative dream of being a therapist. This was very heart wrenching. I felt like such a failure. As a child, I had so many dreams and goals that I wanted to accomplish, and I thought I could do anything I put my mind to. Now I had concluded that I was just one big loser.

I kept on deliberating why God was doing this to me. I couldn't understand why He was causing so much suffering to occur in my life. I began to lose my faith to the point where there was hardly even the tiniest amount left. It was too hard to understand why a being so great as God would let my life take such a sharp downward turn. All I wanted to do was be a successful and productive member of society. The money didn't matter. I measured success by how much I helped others. I wanted to do such great work in this world for God, and now I was blaming Him for everything that was out of place in my life. It was very difficult and very challenging, not accomplishing my initial goals. But surely, this phase of my existence would not be the most grueling stage in my life. That was yet to come in time.

Chapter 10

SUCCESS—TO SOME DEGREE

May 2002—December 2003

Just five days after my graduation from college, the unthinkable happened. She died at just the age of 60 years old. My Aunt Betty had been suffering physically since just after my grandmother's passing on May 20th, 2000. My grandma's death from congestive heart failure had been incredibly difficult. I would visit her often, especially during her final years, since she lived only two houses away from my parents' house. I would bring her shakes from McDonald's and broccoli cheese soup from Tim Horton's, because she never ate much and I was worried about her. She was getting very ill, but I never imagined that she would die. Death was the furthest thing from my mind, because I thought she, like everyone else I loved, was immortal. Death wasn't something I thought could happen to her. The truth was that I never could comprehended death or any part of it. I didn't understand how someone I loved could just cease to exist.

Anyways, I was disheartened at her funeral, but managed to give a wonderful eulogy on her behalf. All I knew was that I missed her and that she was gone. I recall asking my Aunt Betty if she was going to get sick and die like my grandma. Her response was, "I don't plan on it. I plan to be around for a very long time." But that promise would prove to be very short-lived.

My Aunt Betty got ill just a couple months after my grandmother's passing, and she had to have her gallbladder removed. At the time of the surgery, they found out that she had extensive liver damage. This was hard to understand because my aunt was not a drinker. If fact, I don't think I had ever seen her take a drink at all. She was later diagnosed with liver failure due to an autoimmune disease. She got sicker and sicker at an extremely rapid rate. Her skin turned yellow, and she was having massive diarrhea, vomiting, and many other symptoms, but she rarely complained. She was a strong, independent woman, and I knew she had intended to keep it that way. Due to the excessive buildup of ammonia in her system, she began to suffer from a severe mental decline. She could hardly think anymore, like a thick fog had descended over her head.

Once, after getting sick, she went to her doctor in a close neighboring city and never returned home. We couldn't find her anywhere, and this was very unlike her reputable character.

It turned out that Betty had gotten lost in the local area, and had ended up miles away. Hours later, she finally found her way home. But when she arrived, she was out of her mind. This very intelligent, sophisticated woman, who was a financial analyst at Ford Motor Company, had literally lost her ability to think. Not knowing what else to do, I tried to help her with her work. I learned very quickly, with her instruction, how to do the reports. Despite my help, she was forced to retire anyways. I believe that her mental decline was much harder for her to deal with than her physical decline.

During her sickness, she had said in front of me and my mother, who was her sister, that she wanted to give me, my brother Ronald, and my sister everything. My aunt's reasoning for this was because the three of us were on social security benefits and she wanted to make sure that we were taken care of once she departed from this world. Aunt Betty would always give us the things we needed, and when she was around, we were never without anything. But instead of agreeing to my aunt's wishes, my mother tricked my aunt, whose mental state was very weak, into making herself the sole beneficiary on her estate. It totaled nearly one million dollars! I felt extremely betrayed by my mother for doing this. It was a very greedy and unethical thing to do.

I took care of my aunt, even to the point of wiping her butt. Aunt Betty was so sick, so gravely ill, and it was hard to watch her fade away so quickly. Her decline frightened me, and I began to wonder if she indeed was going to die like my grandma had. I didn't know what I would do without her, as she meant the world to me. She had always been there for me. As a child, she took my siblings and I to countless interesting places, and she would entertain us constantly. She always bought us things to the point of almost being overly kind and generous. But all her good qualities couldn't keep her alive, and she departed this world on May 10th, 2002. God had called her home. I reasoned that He must have had special plans for her in Heaven. But her death was very much a tragedy. Very sad. Very emotional. But, like I had done at my grandmother's funeral, I gave a eulogy at my aunt's as well. She passed away less than two years after my grandma's death.

Death was a very hard thing for me to grasp. But the deaths of these two very important people in my life made me question my own mortality. It made me seriously question the purpose of life and all the uncertainties that came with it. It made me take a long, hard look at my own life. If they could die at any time, then so could I. Death scared me to an extraordinary level, and suddenly

I knew I didn't want to die anymore. I wanted to live. I wanted to strive. And even though I hadn't become a doctor or even a therapist, I did have a purpose on this Earth. I could help others, just in a different way. Sure, I wanted things for myself, but perhaps that's not what God had planned for me. Perhaps He had a whole different plan entirely.

As I watched my aunt's coffin lowered into the ground, I thanked God that He had not chosen to take me during my past suicide attempts. I thanked God for my life. I also prayed for Him to take good care of my aunt and my grandmother. As the tears rolled down my face, I knew in my heart, that everything was going to be ok. Maybe not today, but perhaps tomorrow, or even the next day. All I could do was carry on and never give up hope.

After my aunt's death, I applied to many different agencies for a case-management position. I had several interviews and a few months later, I was hired by two different companies within a couple days of each other. One job was working for a foster care agency with vulnerable children and their families, and the other was working with mentally ill older adults. I didn't know what to do. Surely, I hadn't expected to be hired by **TWO** different companies. I then had to make a very critical choice. I eventually made the decision to work with the mentally ill elderly population. Besides, not only was I good with the elderly, I had much personal experience with the mentally ill.

My first day at my new job was very tough. In fact, it was difficult the whole three years I was there. It was very stressful and emotionally draining. I had an extremely large caseload to tend to, and the previous case managers had not even left a dent in the work from numerous years before. I was working very long hours and even on many weekends.

After the first week, I began to feel some level of fulfillment and reward from my job. I was helping others, and that was just what I had planned to do with my life. I was now a case manager. I oversaw clients' cases and made sure they got everything they needed, from physical health treatment to mental health treatment. I was the one who also got the benefits for my clients including social security and medical insurances, such as Medicaid and Medicare. I was making a huge difference in the lives of all my very vulnerable clients. My clients noted this and so did my boss and coworkers. I was enjoying being so useful and so productive. Things were good.

Three months after I began my job, I moved out of my parents' house and into a new home with my brother Ronald. As work life became more and more stressful, so did home life. He was very difficult to live with, because he was also suffering from a severe mental illness. It was nearly impossible for me to hold a conversation with him. All he seemed to want to do was pace the floor and stare absently into space. He never did anything that was worth doing. He would stay home all day and do utterly nothing. He also said hardly anything to me or anyone else. Ronald isolated himself and refused to leave the house. Basically, he was unable to care for himself due to excessive paranoia he was experiencing. So, my mother visited often to help him with whatever he needed.

I was very lonely at this point. I felt like I had no one to talk to or hang out with. I only had work friends. So, I attempted to find a girlfriend online, like I had done in the past. I even met a few of these women. But it became very difficult to hide these relationships from my family. My mom lived only a couple miles away, and I knew how she felt about homosexuals and their lifestyles. I remember making up excuses to where I was going. But I knew I must follow my heart, despite anyone's feelings about what I chose to do with my own life.

I met a woman online and we hooked up for two days. She was my second experience with a woman. I was 23 then, and all I remember is her getting drunk in the hotel room and acting eccentric. To tell you the truth, and I ALWAYS will, I don't even remember her name. It just happened, and that was that. That occurrence led me to the conclusion that I wanted love much more than sex. I wanted to find true and lasting love. Sex should only be an extension of love. Without love, sex is just a physical act. But if you are in love, and make love, you will find a very strong emotional connection, an ultimate bond between two hearts. That was what I desperately hoped and longed for.

This year was filled with going to work and dealing with my mentally ill clients, and then coming home and dealing my schizophrenic brother. I also was trying to deal with my own mental health issues. It seemed like so much insanity was going around. Mental illness was just too much of a common factor in every aspect of my life. It had somehow taken over and now I was left to deal with the consequences of it. I was strong though, and I do believe that being a productive member of society was very good for me. I liked work and it gave me something important to look forward to. But I knew that I needed something else in my life as well. Something was missing.

I lacked a relationship. I wanted someone to share my life with. I needed someone to love and be loved by. But I didn't know where I could find her. I wondered where she was and if she was looking for me too. There were so many questions that I needed answers to, and until I found the solutions, I knew that the loneliness within my heart would continue to linger.

Chapter 11

FINDING TRUE AND UNCONDITIONAL LOVE

December 2003—June 2005

Many times, I would quietly sit and marvel about love, true and lasting love. I wondered what it truly was, and why I yearned so badly for it. I concluded that love is a feeling. It is a very strong emotional bond between two very similar hearts. A soulmate is the one and only person who you can connect with completely on all levels—mentally, emotionally, and physically.

I was looking for my life companion, but I never expected that I would ever find the one who would complete me forever. I never thought that I would find the one who I could fall so deeply in love with. But despite my impression that I would never find the love of my life, I was about to. My life was headed for a very positive transformation. I had a decent job, which I was very satisfied with. And now, I was going to have a wonderful love life filled largely with romance and passion. My life was about to become so magnificent that I would barely be able to tolerate it, and I couldn't comprehend why something this good was finally going to happen to me. God was about to answer all my prayers. I don't even know if I was ready to have something this wonderful and life changing happen to me, but it was about to.

This next year and a half of my life would be the best, most exciting, most exhilarating, and most satisfying time of my life. I would be the happiest that I had ever been in my entire life. I would feel exulted and in high spirits. Now, I am about to share this incredible experience of devotion with you. . .

It was the first week of December 2003 that I found it. I saw a newspaper with personal ads in it that was just lying on the chart cabinets at my place of work. Being inquisitive, I eagerly picked it up. I did not know what I would find, if anything at all. But I did find something. It was a phone number for a relationship hotline. After many failed attempts of trying to find a suitable woman on the internet, I decided I would give this a shot. After all, it couldn't hurt to try. I was so desperate, at this point, to find someone to love. I thought that this could possibly be the answer to my incessant prayers.

So, after I got home from work that day, I made the call that would change my life forever. It started off simply as curiosity. I heard the first woman's voice message that she had made to try to sell herself to an individual for a relationship, and I found myself disgusted by what she had to say. Her recording was all about sexual things and this really turned me off. So, I moved on to the next woman's message, and the instant I heard her beautiful, soft-spoken voice, I knew. I felt this complete utter rush fill me, and that is when I knew that she was the one. I listened intently to her message that spoke of love, commitment, and a desired long-term relationship. I loved her voice and everything she had to say. She communicated that she was 33 years old and was looking for someone at least 25 years old. I was only 24 at the time, but I was hoping she would still give me a chance. I listened to her voice again, because it was hard to believe what I was hearing and what I was feeling inside. I then listened to her message a third time. Then I felt compelled to respond to her relationship hotline ad. I left a message but was so nervous that I forgot to send it. Something was stirring deep within me. I called again, and tried another time, but couldn't remember if I pressed the button to save it. So, I tried a third time, and decided that if it hadn't worked this time, then perhaps it just wasn't meant to be.

Over the next couple weeks, I thought about her and hoped she would call me. I even tried to find her message on the phone hotline again just to hear her voice once more. I sat impatiently and waited, dreaming of finally finding true love. I assumed that maybe she wasn't interested in me because she thought I was too young for her.

Christmas came and went that year with no return call from her, so I gave up. I felt totally defeated when it came to love. I concluded that maybe I would never find love. Secretly though, at least in my heart, I was encouraging myself to keep the hope and the faith. For the next several days, I prayed constantly to God and trusted that He would answer my prayers.

So, it would be. Love would finally be. I knew this completely in my heart and in my soul, when I received a call from that sweet and familiar voice on December 29th, 2003 at about 6:30pm. The instant I heard the voice on the other end of the line, this incredible feeling surged throughout my body. I was a little nervous at first, but I almost instantly relaxed and felt completely comfortable talking with her. It was almost like she was an old friend. We talked and talked about ourselves and our dreams and our hopes and about what we wanted in a relationship. We connected so fast and so powerfully.

After the first hour of talking, I knew that we would surely be friends at the very least. After the third hour had passed, it felt like I had finally met my best friend. And after the sixth hour of talking that wonderful night, I knew I was in love. I just felt this intense passion and urgency stirring inside of me. There was so much intimacy already. At the six-and-a-half-hour mark, we started talking about making love. And to tell you the truth, I felt completely comfortable talking to her about it. It didn't feel inappropriate or the least bit disgusting as it had with others. It felt like this was just another part of growing closer to her. I wasn't ashamed to speak of sexual acts with her. It just felt so right. To me, making love was just a part of life, love, and devotion. When we finally decided to end our conversation at the eight-hour mark, we said good night and we told each other "I love you". It was so dang incredible. I have never, even to this day, been as close to anyone as I was to her.

We talked over the next several days. We grew even closer, if that was at all possible. Then we made the decision to meet in person on January 3, 2004. We talked on the phone as I made the hour drive to her apartment. A feeling of excitement stirred inside my soul at the thought of meeting her in person. I was so damn elated. I felt great. I wouldn't call it mania. It was just a feeling of extreme anticipation and incredible longing.

As I pulled into the parking lot, she waved at me from her forth story balcony. Wow! There she was, the woman of my dreams. I was so eager to meet her, even though we just met by telephone less than a week earlier.

Katie came running out of the apartment building and across the parking lot. My first thoughts, when I saw her, were that she was too old for me and not very good looking. But I knew that looks were insignificant, so I put that useless thought away deep in my brain.

When she arrived at my car, she jumped on me and started kissing me passionately. My God, that was so great. And I felt like I wanted, no needed, her love. We stood there kissing in the parking lot for like five whole minutes. Her kisses were intense and very passionate. I wanted her so bad in an emotional and physical way.

After we temporarily stopped kissing, I took five gifts out of my car—one for each of Katie's five senses. I believed that the way to a woman's heart is through her senses. I thought that you must satisfy each of the senses to please a woman. I gave her red roses for the sense of smell. I provided a camera, to take pictures of her and I together, for sight. I then bestowed upon her a premium candy bar for taste. I then handed her a CD that had our song on it—A

97

Moment Like This by Kelly Clarkston—for the sense of hearing. And finally, I gave her an angel teddy bear for the sense of touch, but then I commented to her that I would like to be her gift of touch. Katie smiled adoringly, and we strolled along together hand in hand into her apartment building.

We resumed making out in the elevator. It felt so good and so right. Then we went into her apartment. I hadn't expected anything at this point, but I went with my feelings, as we continued making out on the couch. I started sucking on her neck and found out that she really liked this, and of course, she returned the favor. I craved for more but I decided that I had to do the right thing first. Before we were to make love, I knew I had to propose to her. So, I stopped her and told her we needed to go to the mall and get to know each other better. She reluctantly agreed, not really wanting to stop the extreme passion between us.

At the mall, we took pictures in a photo booth, and had some lunch together. We talked and talked. I remember how she smiled at me. I felt this intense and incredible bond forming between us. We went into a jewelry store and I told her to pick out any engagement ring that she wanted. Katie picked a yellow gold ring in the shape of a heart with diamonds in it. It was beautiful, much like she was. She agreed to marry me with no hesitation whatsoever, but back then same-sex marriages were not legal. That didn't matter, because we would be married in our hearts and in our souls.

Upon returning to her apartment, we made love repeatedly. I craved for her touch. I desired to know every part of her body, as I felt that I already knew so much of her mind. It was the best sexual experience that I had ever had up until that point. It was perfect, breathtaking, and amazing. Repeatedly, we brought each other to the point of climax. We were so severely exhausted, and the hours seemed to go by so fast.

The next morning, I spontaneously suggested that we get matching tattoos. She agreed whole-heartedly. We picked out a heart tattoo with a rose through it. The heart had a banner on it. The one to be permanently exhibited on my body read "Katie" and the one displayed on her body recorded my name.

Katie went first, because I was afraid if I went first, she'd freak out on me and not get her tattoo. I remember holding her hand as they placed the tattoo on her left breast over her heart. It looked very painful, and she was squeezing my hand tightly. I never had a tattoo before, but I reminded myself that I was doing this as an act of love and commitment to the woman of my dreams. After about an hour and half, we both had matching tattoos. I felt that this was a very special and intimate thing that we had done. We had sealed our commitment to each other.

The next day arrived and it was time for me to leave. I had to go back to work, but I didn't want to go. I wished in my heart that I could stay with Katie forever. My biggest fear at that point was that my mother would find out and end my beautiful relationship with this incredible woman. I was in love, and I wouldn't let anyone ruin this. I would find a way. I always had found a way through difficult situations in the past, and I certainly wasn't going to let this time be any different.

I went back to work in a very elated mood, but inside I was scared. I was frightened, because I knew I had to do something quickly before my mother ended my relationship with Katie. So, Katie and I decided that I would move into her apartment with her. This seemed extreme and very quick, but I wasn't about to lose the woman of my dreams. And so, I consulted my new therapist on the issue and she encouraged me to follow my heart. I was scared because I knew my family would disown me and I would lose them, but if they refused to accept me, then perhaps they weren't worthy of being a part of my life.

In January 2004, I moved in with Katie, just five days after meeting her in person. Despite following my heart, like my therapist suggested, I still felt extreme guilt due to my parents' betrayal. Despite my guilt, I was very happy. In fact, I was happier than I had ever been in my entire life. I was so in love. Most everything seemed perfect except the strained relationship with my family. But regardless of my efforts, it seemed that my family would never accept me. But I knew in my heart that I had to move forward. I had to remain strong.

The following month we moved to a new apartment that was closer to my work. Soon after our arrival in the new town, she began to really miss her autistic son something terrible. Joey was currently living with Katie's mother about an hour away. He had just turned nine. I wasn't sure at first if I was ready for a child, especially an autistic one, but if that meant being with Katie, then I felt it was worth it. Apparently, he was living with his grandmother, because she had taken custody of him, at a time when she felt Katie was incapable of taking care of her own son.

Katie and I wrote vows for each other and we secretly married on January 20th, which was Katie's birthday. The vows were original and heart-felt. It was magnificent being able to now call her "my wife". This made our bond even stronger.

Less than a month after the move, I became concerned about Katie. She was becoming extremely depressed over missing her family. So, I took her to a behavioral center. They talked to her and released her, and after a few weeks, it seemed to me that her depression had lifted.

I didn't want to take Katie away from her son, so we would visit her family, including her son, every other weekend. Katie, Joey, and I would go to the mall and play in the arcade and have pizza. Her family seemed accepting of me and they treated me with respect and dignity. Not only did I have a wife, I now had a son. It was incredible.

As our relationship continued over the next several months, I would go to work and then have someone to come home to who cared deeply for me. It was so nice to not be alone anymore, and to have someone who loved me unconditionally. We spent every moment, that I wasn't at work, together. She even helped me at work on some

Saturdays. Katie didn't have a job or a car, but that didn't matter. I loved her.

I discovered so many incredible things about Katie. She was loving, kind, considerate, passionate, romantic, understanding, compassionate, and she appreciated me and everything I did for her. I would go to work in the morning, after our passionate nights of love making, and be in the most incredible mood. Everyone noticed how happy I had become. I felt so complete. The emptiness was gone.

In July 2004, I purchased a new car. Due to the car payment, I noticed I was getting too much in debt. I owed like $1000 on my credit cards. (I had a whole collection of them!) I knew I had to do something to earn some extra money, because I wanted to bring Joey home to Katie and me. We had even rented out a larger apartment expecting Joey to come home to us.

I surfed the internet, hunting for a way to earn some much needed, extra cash. I was looking for a work at home opportunity, so that I could stay at home and help Katie with Joey. I was ready for a family, besides Joey was her blood and they deserved to be together. I would do anything to make Katie happy and this, I felt, was the best way.

So, I considered an eBay business, and decided that I would give it a shot. I would open an eBay store. I was so excited, and I was convinced it would work. In fact, I thought that there was no way it could fail. After all, I had become Valedictorian against all odds.

So, in November 2004, I opened my business, which I named "Best Quality Items". My motto was "It makes sense to only pay cents for high quality items". I worked hard and long hours on my business after my case manager job and on weekends. Sometimes I would work all night. I was determined to the point of all-out mania. And despite telling Katie that I was doing this for her and our family, she became very frustrated with me. She would want me to come to bed with her, and I would refuse, thinking that I had to work continuously throughout the night on my business. I knew that if I didn't succeed, we wouldn't be able to afford to bring Joey home, and that is what I thought Katie wanted more than anything.

So, I bought tons of items in bulk and attempted to resell them. No luck. I ended up spending thousands of dollars and only recouping like $100. I didn't want to be a failure, so I continued to buy more and more, determined to find an item that would sell big. My thoughts were racing. I was getting hardly any sleep. I was pushing myself so hard and it wasn't working. I believed that I would have to push myself even harder. I wouldn't let myself stop and relax, until I had achieved the highest level of success.

The intense stress I was putting myself through was leading to a severe mental breakdown. And it literally would. Over time my perfect life would fall apart. I wasn't prepared for what was about to come after I had experienced the good life. All I wanted was to be perfect, and being perfect was what I felt would lead to my inner happiness.

Having a good job and being with the love of my life would soon come to a bitter end. I was about to lose it all. I would rapidly fall, and this time I would never be able to get back up again. Soon, my life would change for the worst. It would be transformed into a black spiral of downward despair and darkness. I wasn't ready for it at all.

Chapter 12

MY FIRST MAJOR PSYCHOTIC BREAK

June 2005—November 2005

By June, I had drained myself of all the existing energy I had left within me. I was weak and weary. I had pushed myself so hard just to make my online business work. I felt that it had to work, because I must make money to bring Joey home to live with us. Katie wanted him home, and I wanted to have a family with her. But despite my longing to be successful with the online business world, I was failing miserably. My obsession with striving for unobtainable success only caused Katie and I to grow distant from each other. She wanted to spend more time with me and I wanted that too, because I really did love her so much. But I felt I had to remain entirely focused on formulating a flawless business.

Also in June, after several months of withdrawing emotionally from Katie, Katie received a phone call from her mom saying that her son, Joey, needed her to come back home. I was shocked and scared that I was losing Katie, and I didn't want that to happen. Maybe she was just going home for a visit, but I feared and worried that she was leaving me for good. As my moods fluctuated, I began to think that she would never come back and that I would lose her forever. I felt my life beginning to shatter into many tiny pieces.

So, the night before she left to go home to her mother and son, we made this incredibly passionate love. I hoped that this would be enough to keep her from leaving me. I needed her to know how much I loved her and didn't want her to leave me.

Perhaps it was just the psychosis setting in, but my mind kept thinking many fearful thoughts. I was becoming very irrational and illogical. I was becoming senseless due to extreme stress and sleep deprivation. Afraid of losing her, I called 911 and told them it was an emergency. When a cop arrived, I tried to tell the officer how much I loved Katie and that I didn't want her to leave me. He thought I was acting very foolish. Despite my efforts of trying to make her stay, she still left. She was gone, and even if it hadn't been true, I thought she was gone for good.

I laid alone, despondent and miserable, in the bed that we had shared for over a year. It was the bed that we had made adoring love in so many times together. There were so many memories in that entire apartment. Her leaving, felt like a knife had been thrust into my already bleeding heart. I was afraid to do anything. I just laid there, so down, so depressed. The love of life had left me. I couldn't understand how that could possibly happen. I had tried so hard to make her happy. And now, I was a failure. I was a loser. And I wanted to die, because I was without her existence in my life.

Just hours after Katie left, I had the worst pain that I had ever had in my entire life. It was a shooting, sharp pain in the right side of my head. I literally thought I was having a stroke. Before I knew it, I experienced myself going through a dark tunnel with a light at the end of it. I believed I was dying or was already dead. I began rapidly spiraling through this tunnel and the light was becoming brighter and brighter. I begged God to let me live. I bargained with Him by telling Him that I would stop being gay and live a heterosexual lifestyle. I would say anything not to die. Then I started swirling backwards in the tunnel and I came back into myself. I was not dead. I was surely alive. I laid there, shocked and stunned. I had come back to this world. Then, I fell into a deep sleep.

Upon awakening, I was in a total state of psychosis. Not only was my mental condition tainted, I felt horrible physically. I didn't know what to do or who to call. So, I called 911. They came, but said that I was fine and then left. I remember that I hadn't even locked the door when they exited my apartment. I fell back asleep, only to awaken to the sight of a man and a woman, who handed me an ecstasy pill and a small cup of liquor. They claimed they were the paramedics and that the pill would make me feel better. So, I took it.

The next thing I remember is waking up feeling like I had been raped. My body was so sore. My mind started concocting different things that the perpetrators had said. "Well, if you don't have AIDS or herpes, you do now." "Why don't you just go home to your mother?" "Bitch, all fags get what they deserve!"

Then my mind started coming up with stuff like the condom breaking and me acquiring herpes from the rapist. My whole mind was coming up with all kinds of delusional ideas, and I was trying hard to rationalize each thought so every one of them would seem logical. To this day, I do not know if the rape really happened or not, but now I am being forced to believe that it may have been all in my mind. This was just the beginning of my first major psychotic breakdown.

I began feeling little shocks throughout my body, which I believed were being caused by what I called "proton radiation". Also, I began to totally isolate myself, because I was too afraid to do anything. I thought that everyone was going to kill me, and their motive was simply because of that fact that I was gay. I thought that everyone hated gay people so much that they wanted them all dead. But I couldn't understand why they chose me out of all the homosexuals in this world. I finally decided that they had chosen me because I was so happy with my life and my lifestyle and that they didn't think any gay person deserved to be happy. I began believing that they had secretly planted cameras and microphones in my apartment. I thought they were selling the videos of Katie and I having sex on internet websites. I didn't know for sure who these people were. I thought maybe the N.S.A. (National Swastika Association) were the people attacking me with this proton radiation, which caused me to feel shocks throughout my body. I felt it may be them because this organization tries to convert homosexuals into heterosexuals. They were attempting to convert me by raping me and using this proton radiation, which they shot through my apartment windows at my head and body. It was like a laser that stimulated parts of the brain by sending electrical impulses throughout my body.

I feared that they had installed a device in my car that electrocuted me when I drove it, causing me to have extreme dehydration. Once, I believed that they were filling my apartment with gas through the vents, and I could even smell it. I assumed it was like a gas chamber built to terminate the lives of gays and lesbians. I was so deeply scared. I was in a constant state of distress and alarm. My life was becoming a living horror. I feared for my own mortal existence every moment of every day from June 2005 to November 2005. It was impossible to sleep, causing me to have many additional delusions and hallucinations. I began driving from place to place, trying to escape the people who wanted to see me dead. But no matter where I went they would always follow. I heard their voices everywhere I went. I just could not be still. I could not relax at all. I was so damn petrified.

I began creating even more delusions in my fragile mind. I thought Katie's family and mine were the Hatsfields and the McCoys, two historical families in Kentucky whose chronic quarrel began over a pig. I rationalized everything. I came up with revised family trees and updated my entire life history. Katie and I were the only true Hatsfields and McCoys, as we were both half Hatsfield and half McCoy. We were the only two pure breeds. I came up with the idea

111

that there had been incest within our two families. Our families were tied together in a very primitive way. I had the belief that our families' last names had been changed. My mom was a Hatsfield and my father was a McCoy, while Katie's mom was a McCoy and her father was a Hatsfield. Somehow, I concluded, through intense research on my part, that Katie and I were cousins. Only later to established that Katie and I were really sisters. I resolved that the real reason the perps were after me was because of incest, not homosexuality. The perps were trying to show me something through this proton radiation to my head, which was supposed to alter my brain chemistry.

I went to work one day and told a coworker that my live-in girlfriend was my long-lost sister and that I hadn't even known it. I told my peer that I was staying with "my sister", because I loved her. Once, I even drove to a psychiatric facility to have my mother and aunt admitted for the Hatsfield and McCoy incest scandal, but instead I was the one admitted. I couldn't understand why everyone was against me.

Also, there was the time that I nearly ran my aunt off the road because I believed she was evil. I chased my aunt Michelle right into the nearest police station parking lot. I thought she was guilty of being involved in this extremely complicated scam within our incestual family. After turning my car into the police station, I did a U-turn and promptly left. I was terrified of the cops, because I believed they were going to admit me to mental hospitals. That was the last thing I wanted, because I feared the doctors would kill me there. But it was the thing I needed most. The cops were doing nothing about the perps. They didn't believe anything that I had tried so hard to tell them, but then again, no one did. It really hurts when everyone doubts what you hold deep within your own heart to be true.

I suddenly got a vengeance against my brother Roger, who I believed was guilty of the act of incest against me. I thought he was the one who had entered my apartment and raped me. I believed he was trying to teach me a lesson for being gay. I drove and drove but I was having extreme difficulty remembering where his house was located. I stopped at a store in his neighborhood, stormed inside, and demanded to know where he was at. I explained to them that Roger was guilty of incest within the Hatsfield and McCoy families. They escorted me out of the store for causing a scene, and I never did find his house. After a couple hours of searching, I was exhausted and imaginatively dehydrated from the device in my car that was causing shocks to be surged throughout my body. I really believed that the car was electrocuting me and that I needed water desperately to maintain my life. I felt so drained physically, not to mention mentally. I stopped at the nearest gas station and purchased five liters of bottled water. I guzzled them all down quickly and gave up trying to find my brother.

I eventually found my way home, despite my disorientation. I urinated on myself the instant I unlocked the front door of my apartment. I was home but my unrelenting fears continued. I believed that this apartment would be my final resting place. I began trying to bargain with the perps by speaking, mostly shouting, out loud at them. I could hear them talking to me from the other apartments in the building. They were telling me how evil and disgusting I was for being gay, and they continued to threaten my life. They spoke of wicked and demeaning things, including raping me and murdering me.

Now, my delusion that my mother had sold my eggs became even more genuine. I hated her for doing this. I believed that my eggs and my brother Victor's sperm had been sold to produce red headed babies for a society that had a high demand for them. My mother had made a huge amount of money from this corruptive act. In fact, the amount that I was told by my voices was $1,000,000. I believed that my aunt knew about this, and that had been my justification for chasing her in my car. Also, I believed that my Aunt Michelle had killed my Aunt Betty through giving her tainted medication to ruin her liver. And her motive for doing this was simply greed. At the time, she was guaranteed a large inheritance when my Aunt Betty passed away.

I began believing that people were communicating with me through psychedelic images on my computer. I thought I was reconstructing the story of my life through images and music for the sake of a movie that was being recorded through secret cameras in my apartment. I believed I was going to be a movie star. I also believed that they were going to give me a lot of money in the future. And I knew I needed this money to get Katie back. I missed her so much.

I hid on the floor by my bed to avoid the proton radiation, that was being blasted through the windows, hitting my body. But they always managed to get the shocks through the mattress and into my body. I knew this because I felt it. I was hallucinating the feeling of being shocked throughout my head and body. I believed this proton radiation was a form of electroconvulsive shock therapy (ECT).

They were shocking me to scare me straight. I believed that the laser beams they were using were very powerful. I felt constant shocks throughout my body, especially in my head. I worried that I was going to die from this cruel experiment. I feared dying gravely. I wasn't going to be the one to kill me. The power now belonged to the perps. I was so damn frightened. The voices just continued to mock me, telling me if I didn't turn straight they would kill me with this radiation. All I knew was that I didn't want to die. The whole concept of death was tough and very difficult to understand. I would do anything to survive these criminals, who I believed worked for the government. But deep within me, I didn't really know if I could denounce and suppress my true sexual orientation.

I had nowhere to run and no one to turn to. There was nothing I could do to escape this dreadful situation. No one would listen to my delusional tales. I strived for survival, but in truth it seemed so hopeless. The more time went on, the further and further I grew apart from my wife, Katie. We were still communicating by phone, but I was scaring the shit out of her. I was telling her all my psychotic delusions, which I believed were authentic. I was pushing away the person I loved most in this world. She was incapable of understanding what I was going through, despite her positive quality of being a very understanding person.

I feared Katie had left me permanently. All I thought I could do was I go on a date with another girl and try to start over. Katie called me on the telephone when I was on my way to pick up a blind date. Katie wanted me to go out with her that night, but stupidly, I chose to go on a date with the other girl. I concluded that two sisters shouldn't be in a relationship. Rejecting Katie was ultimately the wrong decision. One I will always regret. To this day, I cannot understand why I would have chosen any person, over Katie, to spend time with.

Going out with someone else, only increased the distance between Katie and me. I couldn't blame her for not wanting to be with me anymore, because of my erratic and unpredictable behavior. But at the time, I could not see that. I believed that unless Katie and I stayed apart, the government would kill us both, and I knew that I could not risk that. I loved Katie and did not want to see her die alongside with me. I had to do the right thing, and being apart from her, I felt, was the right verdict.

With all the stress associated with my severe psychosis, losing Katie, sleep deprivation, and working so hard at both my day job and my online business, I felt forced to go on medical leave from work. I spent the time off pushing myself harder and harder, as I worked on my online business for the next few weeks. I cited the reason for my medical leave as "stress". I was later fired from work because my mental condition was not improving. My employer even called the cops once and they took me to the mental hospital, because I feared I was being stalked and that everyone was trying to kill me. That was the first time I was handcuffed, but it indisputably wouldn't be the last.

I would end up psychiatrically hospitalized five times total during this major psychotic breakdown. At the hospital, I feared that they were poisoning me through medication, food, and drinks. I was hearing voices talking to me. They were projecting themselves from an electrical source and through the radio transmitter that they had installed in my back.

I began to fear that the hospitals were now doing electroconvulsive shock therapy on me to turn me straight. I also worried these perps were putting drugs in my cigarettes and in my medications, causing my thoughts to be distorted.

They wanted me to act insane, because it made a great movie.

I realized my situation was crazy and hard for anyone to believe. But in my mind, this was my reality. I believed all these delusions were facts. As for hearing voices, I didn't believe I was. I thought that these voices were coming from real people. After all, I didn't want to believe I had this type of mental illness. I didn't have the impression that I was the crazy one. I believed that I was simply the victim of a horrible and very unusual criminal experiment.

At one psychiatric hospitalization, I believed that I had been injected with a radioactive isotope called barium. The barium was causing psychosis as it decayed into half-lives. It was all part of "the project", which was a movie on how to turn a homosexual into a heterosexual.

At another hospitalization, I arrived at the delusion that I was "the savior of medical science". Somehow, these experiments that they were doing on me, caused me to have this status. I put a towel on my head and draped a sheet around me like someone in Christ's days. I felt God was very close to me. I was going to die just for the sake of helping science determine that homosexuals could not be converted. And it didn't matter how many times their brains were shocked.

I remember seeing a man, who appeared to be a patient, with a needle in his hand. I thought I was going to be executed for the reason of being the one homosexual that refused to be converted. I formulated the notion that I was going to have my last supper, just like Jesus Christ. I remember how slowly I ate that TV dinner that they had given me. I really thought I was on my way out, because I was convinced that the hospital was going to kill me. I heard the voices of the staff and patients saying things about me. But it was all in my mind. At the time, I was not capable of accepting that I indeed had a thought disorder on top of the mood disorder which I had learned to embrace.

During yet another hospitalization, I kept calling 911 on the phone, which was provided for the patients to use. The fear that I was going to die lingered strongly. I thought that this was going to be the end of my life. The end of my mortal existence. I was sure that the doctors were going to murder me. I also figured that my murder would be what would gain me the title of "the savior of medical science".

After many consecutive hospitalizations, I had lost everything. I was in major debt due to a failing business. I had been fired from my case manager job. I had to give my car back to the dealership because I couldn't afford to keep it. I had lost my apartment. But most hurtfully was the hard, sad truth that I had lost my soulmate.

Katie and I had made a last-ditch effort to stay together, by planning to purchase the house across the street from Katie's mother. We were attempting to reconstruct our relationship. I would drive to her house leaving gifts and sending flowers. I wanted her back more than anything. But there was no way that we would be able to afford the home.

During that fateful day in November when we said goodbye to each other, I felt deep within my heart that Katie would always love me. I was at her mom's trailer saying goodbye to Katie, and that is when she promised me that we would always be together, forever, no matter what. But I knew that this was really our last goodbye, because she couldn't look me in the eyes. I could empathetically feel her pain within me. We talked, hugged, and kissed. There would be so many broken promises between us. Then, before I even had a chance to accept this final goodbye, I drove away. It was over. I knew I would never see the love of my life ever again.

After that happened, I knew that I had to accept the fact that I had lost everything, including Katie. She had been my everything. Katie had been my whole life for nearly two years. And now she was gone, and frankly, I felt that I was too. My mind was spinning, and my heart was breaking. It was over. I would never forget her. How could I? How do you forget and move on after losing the most important person in your life? How do you heal after that? And to this very day, this is the one thing in my life, that I can honestly say, I will never be able to mend from. . .

After losing my apartment, I reconciled with my mother and moved back into my old home that I shared with my brother Ronald. I was still very much psychotic. I remember thinking the neighbors were going to kill me by shooting me with rifles through the windows. I had seen the guns. This fear would only be intensified when I heard someone on the roof and saw a man pointing a rifle at me through the skylight in my bathroom ceiling. After he tapped his weapon on the glass, I looked in the direction of the noise and saw the gun. I was so paranoid and suspicious of everyone and everything. I told my mother but she didn't believe me. I was so distrustful of everyone now. I felt trapped in my own home. I would either die there or I would die

if I left. The only option was death. I determined
there were no other possibilities, or were there?

Chapter 13

MY NEW HOME—JUST FOR THE MENTALLY ILL

November 2005—November 2011

I arrived, still psychotic and forever heart broken. It stood before me—my new home for the next six years. If I would have known I would be there for so long, I might have chosen a different path. But no other option or opportunity seemed to exist. Besides, this was what my mother wanted. It felt like she always got what she wanted and like I had no choice about anything in my life. I did recognize that I couldn't live alone anymore, because I was too paranoid that I was going to be killed. This constant fear disturbed my ability to function. My delusions and hallucinations continued to affect every part of my life. I was finding it very difficult to operate at all. I had no job, no car, and personally, it felt like I had no future. I didn't know what else I could do, or where I could go to get help. Nothing mattered anyways, because I had lost everything. No one would even take the time to listen and understand my complex story of how and why I had arrived there at Tulip Valley Center. Also misunderstood were the stories of the proton radiation, the experiments, the Hatsfields and

McCoys, and how I was the savior of medical science. No one believed me, and I was the only one who was positive that all of this was real. I could not understand why no one believed me. I felt abandoned. I felt so alone.

Tulip Valley Center was a psychiatric treatment center for the severely mentally ill. It was an inpatient residential facility with a combination of several houses which could place up to 65 residents. Most patients there were suffering from schizophrenia or bipolar disorder. But several others had schizoaffective disorder, clinical depression, or a personality disorder. While a couple had developmental disorders.

At Tulip Valley Center, I heard story after story about mental illness from staff and residents. They talked about their experiences with suicide, self-mutilation, and depression. Those things I understood. But when they talked about mania, I denied to myself and others that I was suffering from that. I didn't believe that I really had any form of mania. But after living at Tulip Valley for a few years, I just sort of accepted the fact that I indeed had endured some manic episodes in the past, including many hypomanic outbreaks.

Of all the things they discussed, I absolutely could not relate to the residents who spoke about

125

hearing voices. I didn't feel that I had any form of schizophrenia. I was convinced that I was too smart to be crazy. I was just too stubborn to accept my true illness as something I really had or would ever have in my life. I would not let myself be a person who would suffer from insanity for the rest of her life. It was this simple--I did not have schizophrenia or schizoaffective disorder. No way. No how.

Being unable to admit my illness to myself, I was therefore unable to accept it. I thought the answer of having schizophrenia was too simple, compared to the elaborate tangled web of delusions that my mind had made up, and insisted were true. Perhaps, it was the fact that I may have schizoaffective disorder, that was harder to deal with than the actual psychosis itself. Whatever was tougher, I don't know.

I felt stuck and trapped. I was at a facility that I did not belong in or fit in. I was the victim of a vicious and brutal attack by people who were trying to change me into someone who is straight. If I didn't change I was bound to be buried six feet deep, and according to the perps, I would burn in Hell. But my own heart kept telling me that if I did die, I would not go to Hell. I was sure that I would enter the eternal realm of Heaven. I was sure that Heaven was a beautiful place, and I knew in my soul that God really did love me.

This whole thing was a hate-crime that only the perps and I could understand. Maybe it was just that no one wanted to take the time to listen and comprehend what I was saying. They were bias towards me, because I was different and they just couldn't accept that.

At Tulip Valley, I ballooned up nearly 100 pounds. I was at a high of 420lbs while there. I was huge. I must admit that I was indeed fat to the point of being extremely morbidly obese. I tried to lose weight, but instead seemed only to continue to gain it. Food was my sole happiness and excitement while I was there. I ate for comfort. Food was the answer to my every problem, or that was just what I thought. My relationship with food was extremely unhealthy. I knew I should change, but I felt there was no point, because I was going to be killed anyways when I left Tulip Valley. And if I was going to die, why not die fat and happy?

I would go through periods of smoking and then quitting. It would be later that I would be told that smoking cigarettes and the psychiatric drug Clozaril don't mix, causing the medication not to work properly. But I liked smoking. When I went home each holiday to my parents' house, I was forced not to smoke. Then I would start back up again when I returned to Tulip Valley Center. This agitated my mental illness causing multiple break-through symptoms.

While at Tulip Valley Center, my relationship with God continued to be a very questionable one. I wanted God in my life, but felt that He did not love me. I believed that if He truly did love me, He would not allow all these bad things to happen to me. And I did not understand why He had chosen me to be the savior of medical science. I did not know why He wasn't bringing just a little happiness into my life. But then I remembered back to age 25, when I was very happy. I had happiness once in my lifetime, so maybe I shouldn't be so greedy. I knew I had to accept whatever future God had in store for me, whether it be an uncomplicated and pleasant life or a path as difficult as being the redeemer.

I remained at Tulip Valley Center for such a long length of time, because I was unable to comprehend the fact that I was suffering from schizoaffective disorder. Sure, I knew I had bipolar disorder, but I did not believe that I had a thought disorder as well. I made every effort to convince the staff that I was being targeted for being gay, and that I was not mentally sick. Despite my continued attempts, I never did get them to believe me. They never tried to explain to me what was happening to my mind, and even if they had, I'm sure I wouldn't have believed it at that time. My mind had concocted a different truth. I was the target of a cruel medical experiment, and it is that which I chose to believe.

At my place of residency, I was so miserable and saddened to the point of depression. We'd have groups and we'd have menial jobs. Everything they taught us in groups I already knew, and everything they instructed us to do at our jobs, was insignificant. I was getting so bored there and frustrated, because I didn't belong. I didn't fit in with these crazy people, because I was not insane. The perps were the insane ones, not me. They really were doing experiments on me, and they really were going to kill me. They'd see how real this was when I ended up dead. Then someone would finally believe me. But of course, when that happened, I would be dead.

I began writing a book in my spare time to pass away the long, boring hours. It was about my life and my experiences. On each page, I wrote about my delusions, which I believed were real. I did manage to publish it in 2007, only to have my mom, who had become my guardian, take it off the market. Having a guardian was a terrible blow to my independence and self-esteem. But while at Tulip Valley in the year 2011, I redeemed myself by going to court and obtaining my own guardianship back.

I was highly upset that my mother had ruined my chance of becoming a known author. I was so mad at her, and I felt betrayed. I thought if other people read my story, that somehow the perps would be caught. When she took my book off the market, it felt like she was killing me, because now the perps would not be caught and they would come after me again when I left Tulip Valley. However, I do have to admit, I felt safer at Tulip Valley than I had anywhere else in a very long time.

I was also too stubborn to realize that my delusions were in fact that, delusions. But I knew I had to find a way out of this mental institution, in which I felt trapped and extremely restricted. I knew that if I refused to admit that the proton radiation was not real, I would never get out of this place and be able to move on with my life. I wanted out even though I knew that they would find me and kill me. I had to get out and find Katie again, to spend at least one last night with her. If they were going to kill me, I wanted to die with her by my side. I would stand up for what was right. And that was my crusade of love.

Unfortunately, I had lost touch with Katie during those six years of being institutionalized. The last things that she had told me were that she had found a new girlfriend, and that she didn't love me anymore. Hurtfully, she told me to stop contacting her. I felt confounded. All I knew was that I had to get her back into my life. I remained in love with Katie and was faithful to her the whole time I was at Tulip Valley.

I made the decision to tell the psychiatrist what she wanted to hear, even if it meant lying. I told her that the proton radiation and other thoughts I was having were not real, and that they were delusions caused by a mental illness. I told her I knew I had schizoaffective disorder. I then praised the medication, and explained to her that I understood that I needed to take it for my whole life. Sure enough, it worked, and after over six years of a meaningless and nothingness existence, I was deemed ready to move on with my life.

I had no idea what to do next. There were so many decisions to make, and I knew that freedom would demand responsibility. I did know that I wanted to find an apartment, get a job, and get a car. But the most important thing was to find Katie first, and I would never stop until she was back in my life.

I was unsure if I ready to be released. In my mind, being released was equated to a death sentence. I alleged, with every fiber of my being, that I would be executed for standing up for my sexual orientation, as soon as I got out into the community. Despite telling my psychiatrist that I was having delusions, I did not actually believe that I was delusional. I just wanted out of Tulip Valley. I would have to be ready to face this big evil world again, just one little step at a time.

Chapter 14

STARTING OVER

March 2012—June 2014

I found a roommate online and I moved in with her, without giving it even a second thought. It turned out to be the wrong move because she ended up being an alcoholic, a drug addict, and a prostitute. Obviously, this situation was extremely unhealthy for me. So, I stayed with my social worker from Tulip Valley, while I made other arrangements as to where I would live. I ended up moving in with my social worker's neighbor, and I stayed there for approximately four months. While there, I tried to gain a little independence by taking the bus to my appointments, and being responsible for making all scheduled engagements.

My weight was quickly rising with each passing day, as I now had the freedom to eat whatever I wanted. I gained about 25 pounds during those four months. I was having trouble just doing the simplest of things, including walking and even wiping my own butt. My unsightly appearance wasn't what bothered me the most. It was my rapidly declining health that really frightened me. My health was failing due to my morbid obesity.

I suffered from high blood pressure, high cholesterol, diabetes, sleep apnea, GERD, etc. The list would continue to become even bigger than it already was. I had been prescribed many medications, and at one time was taking over twenty pills a day. I was told by multiple doctors that if I didn't lose weight, I would surely die.

Then I was diagnosed with pseudotumor cerebri, which is a swelling of the brain that causes fainting among other symptoms. This required me to endure a total of five spinal taps to withdraw the excess fluid. These were extremely painful. In addition, my excess weight was causing my feet to break repeatedly, and they were very resistant to healing. The truth is that none of this phased me to any degree. I loved food so much that I continued to eat anything and everything I wanted. If the perps were going to kill me, at least I'd die happy. When your dead, it doesn't matter how much you weigh.

After wearing out my welcome at this lady's house, I moved into my own apartment. I was two hours away from my family and I chose to have it that way. I knew my family would try to take away my right to be gay, and would ruin any future relationships that I may have.

After moving in, I bought pizza almost every day and ate nonstop to numb my internal pain. I grew to an enormous weight of nearly 500 lbs. I acquired COPD at that point, because my lungs were too small to support my huge body. I was placed on oxygen because I couldn't do the simple, taken for granted task, of breathing, anymore.

I began attending overeaters anonymous, which I really didn't feel was helpful. But I did make a few friends there. One of my new friends introduced me to her mother in law, who ended up becoming my caregiver. I was no longer able to care for myself and my needs. I was slowly losing my independence.

One friend told me about her bariatric surgery, and then she introduced me to the doctor who would eventually do my surgery. I was told I was a candidate for the sleeve gastrectomy, but that I would have to lose weight first. Instead of losing weight, I just continued to gain it. One doctor had refused to do the surgery, saying I was too high risk. A second doctor, who I believed saved my life, attempted the surgery on November 3, 2013. It was successful and I dropped thirty-three pounds in just the first ten days!

The total recovery period, from the surgery, was almost a full month. During this period, my caregiver, Mary, took care of me. She shopped for me, cleaned my apartment, and did all my other chores. Mary helped me with anything I needed, and I grew quite dependent upon her. Mary told me the story of how her daughter had been very sick and died an early death, at just the age of forty. I felt like she kind of thought of me like a daughter. All I knew was that I needed her help, and that she was nice to me and treated me with the respect that I deserved.

After just one year I had dropped almost 200lbs. I was feeling myself fade away, and I could move a lot easier now. I had a lot more energy, and my clothes were becoming much looser. I was getting unsightly hanging skin, but I was also getting considerably healthier, which I felt was the most important thing. I stopped needing to use an oxygen tank, and this was a huge deal for me. I also was miraculously "cured" from my many diseases, including diabetes, high blood pressure, high cholesterol, sleep apnea, COPD, and pseudotumor cerebri. I was taken off all the medication I had been prescribed for those things, and also off a med for angina. I no longer needed to rely on my CPAP machine. I was feeling great with so much added and needed energy. I was feeling on top of the world, and on top of my game. I didn't feel hungry anymore, and just a little food was enough to fill me up. I was terrified, due to my mother's comment, that if I ate too much, my stomach would explode. I knew I wanted to live, not die.

Speaking of dying, it had been a while since I had thought of the perps. I believed that they were leaving me alone, because I hadn't been actively pursuing a relationship with a female. Feeling relieved by their absence, I was finally going to get my life straightened out. First, I needed a decent job, but I didn't know how I would get to work without a car. I thought that maybe I should try starting another online business, and I would refuse to let myself fail this time. I began studying how to successfully sell products through advertising with online videos. It was really very complicated, and I pooled all my time and extra energy into attempting to achieve this goal. I worked and studied these business concepts all day and all night. I felt my mind beginning to slip away, as I was overexerting myself way too much. This situation was seeming all too familiar. It was the cause of my fall in 2005, and it would be the cause of my deterioration beginning in 2014.

Chapter 15

THE FALL OF GRACE

June 2014—March 2015

As the stress in my life continued to increase, I began to falter. I was screwing up my sleep cycle, by working intensely on my computer all day and all night. I was striving for an unrealistic goal, but would do anything to be successful. About two months after beginning my business, I started sleeping during the day-time hours. I was getting very depressed over the fact that I had slaved over this business and it was not yet fruitful. I wanted this so bad, because I figured it would make me a productive member of society who earned her own money. The truth was that I wanted, or perhaps needed, just to be someone, anyone, in this incredibly demanding world.

It was hard to accept the inevitable demise of my internet business. Realizing that my second attempt at creating a successful business had failed, I got more and more depressed. As my disappointment increased, I took more and more to my bed. I was giving up. I concluded that I would never be anyone. I felt that my life would continue to be a catastrophe, despite my few successes in life, which included a weight loss at that time of almost 200 lbs.

Depression arose within me like a dark storm cloud, perhaps identical to that of a tornado funnel. I was isolating myself and wallowing in self-inflicted pity. I felt alone and lonely. It was at times like these that I missed my ex, Katie, so much. I wanted her to be part of my life again. She was someone I could talk to, and someone I could love and be loved by. I found her information online and attempted to contact her, but she did not respond to any of my emails, letters, texts, or calls. So, I gave up on that too, even though I knew my heart would never, ever, give up on her.

Nothing in my life seemed right, and I had nothing. The feeling of loneliness lingered constantly. I felt like a major disappointment to myself and everyone around me. I had no idea how to solve any of my problems. I considered obtaining a different job, but I still did not have a car, so that idea was discarded. Anyways, I would never have been able to hold a job. I was too far gone to be respectable at any type of work.

I lied in my bed 24 hours a day, only to get up to use the bathroom and get food, which I would consume in my bed also. I wasn't taking showers, because I feared being videotaped naked. I was drinking tons of fluid including soda pop and sports drinks, because I believed I was being electrocuted and needed constant hydration. I was also smoking cigarette after cigarette, totaling nearly three packs each day. I was doing nothing, except existing.

This is when the voices entered my life again and took hold, causing severe and multiple delusions. In addition, I was hallucinating, and it was affecting all five of my senses. My mind was slowly disintegrating. Things were not right at all within my mind. After either my psych meds were adjusted or I missed a dose, I became terrified and paranoid of everyone and everything. Perhaps the paranoia was just a break-thru symptom caused by stress. But whatever its cause, it was very apparent in my behavior.

I remember I got a huge headache that was like the one I had in 2005, only worse. It had been the indicator of the start of my breakdown then and I feared another decline. My past delusion, that "they" were doing electroconvulsive shock therapy on me, resurfaced. This time I believed it occurred through the walls and ceiling, not the windows. They were sending shocks into my brain and body, and I began to feel, see, and hear these shocks! I assumed that the "medical researchers" were the people who were doing this scientific experiment on me.

The experiment was supposed to have begun in 2005, when I signed a long contract at the doctor's office, and was scheduled to end ten years later. In the year 2005, I believed I had been injected with Barium, which is a radioactive isotope. It has half-lives as it breaks downs. This element was supposed to be in my system for a full 10 years, after which time, I would die. Apparently, according to the voices, I had given them permission to do these experiments on me and to end my life after the 10 years were up. The Barium was somehow able to allow the medical researchers to read my mind when taking "x-ray images" of my brain through the walls of my apartment.

One of the medical experiments that they were doing on me was what the voices called "the cancer project". I believed they were finding all the cures for every type of cancer and many other illnesses through using me as a human guinea pig. My mind had concocted a list of twenty or more real diseases that they had cured through my assistance. They used the key, which they had gotten from management, to enter my apartment at night and take samples of my tissues and cells.

I was sure that my body was being used to find cures for cancer and other diseases.

I was unaware of the medical researchers' presence in my apartment because I was being poisoned with carbon monoxide through the ventilation system. I believed I was chosen for this project because I had the blood type O-, which is the universal type. I knew that my former employer was involved and was getting a huge payout because of their involvement. That's when I began to demand payment from the medical researchers for using me. I began shouting at them throughout the day and night.

I believed the medical researchers were breaking into my apartment when I had doctor appointments or had to go grocery shopping. They were tampering with my medications, doing some sort of experimental chemotherapy on me. Also, I concluded that these "doctors" were doing experimental radiation therapy on me through the shower walls for the colon cancer, which I believed I had. I thought these experimental drugs and experimental radiation were going to kill me before the end of my contract. If not, I would surely be killed anyways when the contract was terminated.

Due to the belief that these drugs would kill me, I stopped taking all my prescribed medications. At one point, the voices were telling me that the medical researchers had cured me of all my diseases and that I wasn't supposed to take my meds anymore because they would affect the results of their testing. And if I did take my meds as they had been prescribed, the voices told me that they would kill me through the walls and ceiling using their ECT.

The medical researchers were communicating constantly with me through the unwelcomed voices in my head. I believed these voices were the actual voices of the medical researchers who I believed lived in my apartment building. I believed I could hear their voices because I had the gift of "super-sonic hearing", which was being agitated by the electrical shocks to my auditory nerves. They could read my mind through the barium that I had been injected with. I would constantly talk, out loud and through my thoughts, with the voices all day and all night long, day after day. The radio transmitter that they had placed in me years earlier was allowing them to hear everything I was saying and doing.

After completing the cancer project, I was immediately placed in my next project. This one I called "the homosexual project". The medical researchers would "shock" different parts of my brain to stop me from being a lesbian. The voices threaten that if they couldn't change me, they would kill me. They bulked that everyone else they had tried it on had been successfully converted into a heterosexual. The medical researchers called sexual orientation "sexual preference", and they were trying to convert all the "fags". The medical researchers wouldn't accept that they had failed on me. I was terrified that if I continued to stand up for what I believed in, that I would have to die for my right to be gay. Each day, I feared for my life. This was one of the scariest times in my life, tying with the psychotic episode that I had endured in 2005.

The third project that I was forced into was the "feeling sensations project." Somehow, they could know my body's response to different stimuli, including hot and cold and even the removal of a tampon or the feeling of a bowel movement. The hot/cold sensation was tested by controlling the hot/cold water temperature in my shower, and by manipulating the air temperature through a "hatch" they had installed in my heating system. I felt the temperatures change in both of those things. I even heard the hatch being installed. They were also raping me during the night, not only to change my sexual orientation, but to know the body's response to sexual assaults.

These projects, which were being filmed, and my impending death were only intensifying my already deep, dark, depression. I believed that there were cameras and bugs installed in my ceiling. I even purchased a bug detector to prove to myself that they were actually there.

I continued to lie in my bed all day and all night, just listening to my radio 24/7. I continued to fear death, and dreaded taking a shower in front of the cameras. I would listen to love songs nonstop and mourn the loss of my precious Katie. Every song became a message about the two of us, and the emotional relationship we had shared. I was still so heartbroken over Katie, even though we had apart for ten long years.

It seemed as if the radio was trying to communicate messages to me. After exhausting hours upon hours of constantly listening to repeated love songs, I decided to turn the station. I found a Christian pop-rock station that I never knew existed. After repetitively listening to this music, I began to believe that God Himself was connecting with me through the lyrics. I got scared and switched back to my favorite love song station. Then my mind began rewriting the lyrics of the love songs to make them even more personal to me. Frightened, I switched back to Christian rock. The songs again became personalized. This time the words were telling me that my mother wanted me to come home. In my mind, I believed the only reason she wanted me to come home was to control me and stop me from my "fortification" with females.

Suddenly, the Christian music was giving me an intense connection with God. I was feeling God's glorified presence deep within my heart and soul. I felt so powerful. I was beginning to feel extremely close to my higher power. I felt exceptionally holy. It was like I was becoming one with Him. It was as if He was converting me into the next Christ, and filling my soul with abundant devotion. He was telling me something through the lyrics of the songs on the radio. My mind was altering all the words, and I was having a hard time figuring out what exactly He was attempting to tell me.

I was told by the voice of God that my apartment was built on an old burial ground, in which "evil" people were buried. A few rested under the floor of my bedroom. I began talking to these "dead souls". We seemed to be entertaining each other. Their presence relieved some of my loneliness, while I, a "live soul", entertained them and soothed their boredom from being dead for so long and not having anyone new to communicate with.

The voices began to tell me more and more lies which I gullibly believed. My family's crimes were other vivid delusions in which I assumed were true. Over Christmas-time, I went home to my parents' residence for a week to escape the wrath of the medical researchers, but they followed me. They followed me wherever I went.

I believed my mother was poisoning me through toxins in the bottled water she gave me to drink. I could taste and see the poison in it. Also, my delusion that my mother had sold my eggs to my gynecologist in 1995, intensified to the degree in which I believed I had a total of 256 biological children. I believed, also, that my mom had sold my brother's sperm to create a red headed generation through the fusion of my eggs and his sperm. I believed that the male children that were created through this incestual bond grew up into serial killers at puberty, while the girls became the sweetest people around. The voices discussed how the boys were to be executed right before puberty to stop the area from having massive killings. The prepubescent boys were to be taken away from their families and given the legal injection. When I was on a psych ward, I remember seeing one of my sons. His red hair was the only clue I needed.

I began to believe that the voices I was hearing could possibly be from evil spirits that I had the unique ability to communicate with. I began to assume that the dead souls buried under my apartment building were witches. These witches were haunting me and affecting my sanity. When I was in high school a few gothic students put a spell on me. That really happened, so I thought I was under their spell. I was convinced that I wasn't crazy. I assumed I was possessed. There were "time lapses" in which the witches can take you back to any time and then bring you back to the present. The witches were making videos and watching me from Hell to entertain themselves.

I took a picture of Jesus Christ off my window sill to try to soothe my anxiety. It was a picture that I had never seen there previously. I remember there being a picture of Jesus displayed there but not this one. I assumed that someone had switched the picture of Christ with one of an "evil wicked sorcerer". I believed that this, in fact, was not the real Christ even though the picture said, "Trust in Jesus" on it. It was this picture that was giving the witches the power to attack my mind.

The medical researchers still had a few diseases left to find cures for, that had not yet been found by using me as a human guinea pig. My mind suddenly came up with the cure for AIDS. It was a combination of magnesium sulfate, potassium chloride, and rust. It came so quickly that I knew I had to write it down immediately so I could save people's lives. I picked up the picture of Jesus, which was the closest thing to write on, and I recorded the cure on it. Then a couple other disease cures came to my mind, and I quickly inscribed them on the picture as well.

I began to stare at this picture and write the worst things on it, including "the devil makes people go blind." My mind was racing. I began to think that the picture was too evil to keep because it was surely possessed. It was even able to give me a hysterectomy by shooting its spirit into me. I had to get rid of this "unholy picture", because it was too evil of a possession to keep. I threw it in the trash, notes on it and all. I believed that whoever found it would have to endure the witches' rage. Then I took the Bible into my bed with me, and tried to read it. But the words had changed. It became a guide for witches. My mind had constructed a completely different text for the entire book! It was now the witchcraft manual. Then before I knew it, the book turned back into the real Bible. The voices were telling me that Jesus was just "a beggar they hung to the cross," and that He had done nothing good for the world. They told me that I was the real Christ. Then the voices instructed me to rip up the Bible into tiny pieces, because the Bible was corrupt. So, I did! I was then ordered by the voice of God Himself to be the author of the "true Bible", and to leave the world with a legacy, after I was crucified.

Despite getting rid of the picture, who's power had burned a visible hole in the garage bag, I was still being haunted. This time I constructed the idea that the witches were the members of my family and my caregiver. My family was executing me through the electrical sockets using my brother's electrical engineering knowledge. They were just trying to shock me into coming home. Then I concluded that my family members were the medical researchers themselves and lived in apartment 11. They were the people who were raping me to turn me straight. Then I thought that I had been the victim of childhood incest. I knew that I had to avoid my family at all costs. I was terrified of them, but even more scared of being executed alone. Frightened by this idea, I began to wonder if I should indeed move back home.

The witches continued to plague me without rest. I believed they were now raping me as spiritual beings. I believed they were tying my "periadallas" with surgical tape through an invisible spiritual force. I defined the periadallas as a part of my stomach that allows emptying into the small intestine. Tying this part of the body would cause a person to retain all consumed water and food, and the person would literally "blow up". This was like how my aunt Betty had died when her kidneys failed and she retained tons of water. When I finally got up the guts to take a shower in front of the intrusive cameras, I saw myself blowing up in front of my own eyes! I was so scared because I thought that this was my impending moment of death.

I also saw my cat's eyes bulging out of her head. They were huge and Cindy appeared to be staring intently at me. This frightened me into believing that Cindy was a former witch who had been reincarnated as a cat. Then I believed that my cat was the reincarnation of Katie. I assumed that Katie had died in a fire caused by the medical researchers. They had killed her in what was a "joint project". Her heart had been too weak to endure all the shocks. She either died from a heart attack or in that fire. I remember Cindy's constant companionship. Also, I recall her staring out the window, trying to single out help for her psychotic mom, which was me. In addition, I thought that my first two cats, Precious and Juliet, who were now with my Aunt Michelle, belonged to witches before coming into my ownership.

Another visual hallucination, I sustained, was when my caregiver came over to my apartment, after I returned from a mental hospital, to give me my bag of clothes. Right before my very eyes, she transformed into an evil witch who looked just like a patient who had been in the mental hospital with me. Now, I began to believe that Mary, my caregiver, was really a witch and I concluded that it was her who had placed that evil picture of Jesus on my window sill. It was this picture that caused me to be haunted by the witches, so I became terrified of Mary too!

Then there was the hallucination I had in the hospital ER. I went to the bathroom in a state of total paranoia and psychosis. There is was. I saw it. A colostomy bag was attached to my side. I freaked out!

Besides all the auditory, visual, and tactile hallucinations I was having. I was also having gustatory and olfactory delusions. I was tasting sperm and vaginal fluid. I was smelling sperm and horrid body odor under my arms, not caused by lack of showering.

At the time, I had one friend named Alice, who I met during my stay at Tulip Valley.

Because I was so terrified by the whole situation that I was enduring, I decided to stay at her house for a couple nights, but the voices did not cease. Apparently, the medical researchers had bugged her house too and her car. I still heard them, probably from satellite and through the radio transmitter in my back. At her home, I assumed that they were conducting psychological tests on me to determine if I was ready to become a psychologist. The doctors were testing me to see how I dealt with fear and if I could remain calm in the face of danger. Turns out that I ranked with the top score on calmness in the wake of death. They continued to do their testing on me for the entire two days I was there, nonstop. I recall that there was even testing to check IQ, in which I scored as a genius.

I been to ponder all aspects of my future and what would happen next in my life. I knew that I would just have to wait and see where my life and my impending death would take me. My life was simply a bloodcurdling roller coaster, in which you either jump off and die, or reluctantly continue to ride until it safely stops.

Chapter 16

MY TIME IN HOSPITALS

June 2014—March 2015

These delusions had taken a major toll on my mental state of mind and on my physical well-being. I believed that the medical researchers were going to give me a heart attack through their electrical shocks, and I felt actual chest pains. The pain was probably just a hallucination. Or it could have been caused by my increased blood pressure, which was extremely high because of my constant fear of being killed.

Once, I thought I had completely stopped excreting urine. I went to hospital ER, but nothing was found to be wrong. I thought the patients and the doctors were making fun of me, because I could hear them talking about me behind my back. Doctors scared me, because I believed that they were going to execute me through drugs, in an IV, for being gay. Many doctors thought I was insane but did not place me in a mental hospital at that time.

Another time, I went to hospital after insisting I had colon cancer. This became a constant nagging delusion, one that I received many medical tests for, and had to make many trips to my primary doctor and a specialist for. It had been a complete waste of time and money. The voices, who I believed belonged to the doctors, were saying during an abdominal CAT scan that I had stage II colon cancer. If I wasn't going to die when this ten-year project was completed, then I would surely die from this very painful and deliberating terminal illness. I believed the cause of the colon cancer was the barium injection the doctors had given me ten years prior.

All the friends I had made at Overeater's Anonymous betrayed me when I told them I had colon cancer, so I never returned to the meetings. I believe they had seen my mental decline through my words and actions, and that they feared me. Mainly their fear was due to their inability to understand what was happening to me, because even I couldn't understand it myself. They probably assumed that I was purposefully making up the colon cancer thing just to get attention, which was not the truth at all.

Six more psych hospitalizations would occur between June 2014 and April 2015. During that time, I was repeatedly admitted, time and time again. They would ask me if I was hearing voices and I would tell them "no", because I was so sure that I wasn't hearing voices. I believed that I was hearing real people talking about me, behind my back and to me directly, through my super-sonic hearing. I wasn't crazy. I wasn't having auditory hallucinations. I was really hearing these things and they really did exist. But I didn't know how to explain this to the psychiatrists, because I saw them as the untrustworthy perpetrators of these projects, and I believed that they knew damn well what was going on anyways.

I was hospitalized in June 2014 for the eleventh time in my life. It was then that I was contending that my neighbors were trying to kill me. Their motive was that of a hate crime. I told my psychiatrist this, but that was the only thing I disclosed to him. While there, I endured some medication changes and attended some groups that didn't really seem to help. Being surrounded by "crazies" was difficult. After being hospitalized ten times in my teens and twenties, I had belief that I would never be hospitalized psychiatrically again. I had concluded that I would be a sane person for the remainder of my life, but I was surely mistaken.

During the hospitalization, the voices faded away and I became stable and was released 7 days later. Having quit smoking during my hospitalization, I started back up again, as soon as I was released. I immediately started hearing voices again. I didn't realize that starting and stopping smoking can influence the effectiveness of the antipsychotic medication Clozaril.

The next hospitalization occurred just two months later in August. The cops were called to my house by my neighbors after they heard screaming from my apartment. I had been yelling at the perps telling them to "leave me the fuck alone". I was so paranoid, and I thought that by yelling at them, they would just go away. And I knew that they could hear me. I was hospitalized for two weeks, and then released with another prescription for Clozaril. I started smoking again and relentlessly the evil voices returned. When the voices came back, I insisted that the medical researchers knew I had returned from the hospital and were back to conducting their project. I continued to scream at them all day and all night. I even called 911 several times and told them that the neighbors were trying to kill me. The cops came and called an ambulance that took me away to another psychiatric hospital.

My thirteenth hospitalization occurred in December of 2014. Now, I believed that they were going to literally nail me to a cross. When I was in the emergency room right before the psych admit, I ripped out my IV because I believed that they were going to inject me with a drug to murder me. Also at that time, because I believed that electricity would kill me when I was on the toilet, I peed all over the floor of my room at the hospital. In addition, I believed that the witches were putting tampons into my anus to kill me when I finally would be unable to use the bathroom. I believed that my caregiver, Mary, was my real mother and that she was a witch. I thought that I was Glenda the good witch of the North and that Mary was going to fly me away with her. I strongly believed this to be valid. Mary told me that she was going to fly through the window with some help from the other witches and lift me away on the bed to a new world. But it never happened, even though I had anticipated it. I began slamming my head on the floor as hard as I could, repeatedly, after the voices demanded it. I was then given a "babysitter" because of my disruptive and self-injurious behaviors.

During this time, I made calls to my aunt and my mother. During my call to my aunt, I insisted that she had killed my Aunt Betty through medication in her IV; that she had killed over 500 people in the recovery room at the hospital she worked at by the same method; and that she knew about all my children that were stolen from me through the illegal "snatching" of my eggs. I informed my mom I knew about her selling my eggs, and that I knew she was really a witch. Saying these destructive things to them was pushing them even further away. I realized that I was losing all my friends and the support of my family members. I was becoming more and more isolated. But none of this seemed to matter because I assumed that I would be dead soon anyways. It was very painful to think I would have to die alone with no one by my side. Three weeks later, I was again released from the mental institution.

The medical researchers had taken everything away in my life—my wife, my job, my car, my health, my independence, my family, my friends, and soon they would take my very life. I held hope that they would make it right by giving me something in return, such as money, but despite their promises the compensation never came.

I was once again hospitalized in January 2015. This time I believed that the hospital was going to create a new life for me by giving me a new family and new friends. I had to maintain this hope and keep the faith, because that was all I could do with all this chaos happening around me.

After being admitted into this "dungeon" without my glasses, I was unable to glance into the eyes of the two new friends that the medical researchers had chosen for me. If I couldn't gaze into their eyes, I would not be able to make the

159

connection. I was very upset because I knew that I had missed my chance to obtain this part of my new life.

Then the hospital social worker took me to her office to do the paperwork for my admission. When she started to take notes and interview me, I felt a strong and weird connection—an intense presence. I didn't know if this person was chosen by the medical researchers to be my new mom or my new lover. I thought she was probably meant to be my mom because of the medical researchers' homophobia. I had almost $500 in my purse and because I felt this strong euphoric connection I told the social worker that she could keep it all. Despite my insistence, it was returned to me upon leaving the hospital.

During this hospitalization, I believed that my brain was going to fall out of my broken skull, which had been fractured by the ECT. I thought Dr. Rodney, my immediate psychiatrist, was holding my skull closed with all his might as an invisible being, all while the perps continued to electrocute me through the hospital walls. He even broke his wedding ring while holding my skull together with his "big hands". I even began to believe that Dr. Rodney had been chosen to be my new father.

I was released from the hospital a few weeks later, but my life had not been reinvented as I had hoped and had been promised. I was disappointed, depressed, and a bit angry for that fact. But my real anger was with this project that never seemed to end. They had extended my contact illegally. Maybe that was a good thing because I wasn't dead yet, like the end of the project entailed. But maybe death would have been better than all this disgusting suffering that I was enduring.

The voices, once again, returned and this time with a mighty vengeance. They became very demanding, forceful, and manipulating. They gave me no alternative but to act on their demands. They told me that they would kill me instantly with "shock", if I didn't do exactly as they ordered. During this time, I drank an entire bottle of a prescribed liquid laxative, which caused me to have accidents all over my apartment. I was afraid to take a shower because I didn't want to die in the shower naked. A big fear of mine was dying in the nude.

At my apartment, I ripped an entire Bible to shreds. Also, I put a pill into my ear canal. I also swallowed a whole bottle of Tylenol, after which I lost consciousness for three days. When I came to, my delusions just continued. I believed that my family members were electrocuting me through the electrical outlets, and that I was being raped at night by them. I believed it was all being recorded and sold on the internet in Europe and around the entire world.

The following month in February, I saw yet another psych admission. Convinced that the hospital workers were going to kill me, I locked myself in the bathroom multiple times by wedging trial-sized shampoo and lotion bottles between the lock and door handle. I was so frightened. I saw dense smoke coming through the vents which I believed was gas, which was intended to kill me when I breathed it into my lungs. I believed that I was being struck in the head with high voltage shocks through the lights, and that these shocks were going to kill me. I thought I was becoming dehydrated from this "electricity". So, while I was hiding in the bathroom, I frequently drank water out of the toilet using a paper cup from the dining room. Because of the belief that I was constantly thirsty and couldn't leave the bathroom, which didn't have a sink, I felt I had no other choice for survival.

At this hospitalization, like all the rest, I would scream loudly at the voices. I began to believe in something my mind called "miracle magic". And I was told by my "masters" never to repeat that word if I wanted to live. But I didn't care anymore. If they were going to kill me, then they might as well get it over with. Miracle magic was a new form of medical science that was corrupt. I had to let the world know about it, even if it meant dying for what I believed in. So, I started to verbalize the words "miracle magic" repeatedly out loud. I remember that the attending nurse told me that she had been "saved by miracle magic". That was not a good thing to tell a psychotic individual and it only increased my belief that such a thing really did exist.

Looking back on it, and other experiences I have had, I can see that many of the doctors and nurses, not to mention the patients, were not at all very understanding of psychotic people. They were almost to the point of making fun of them and laughing at them behind their backs and even to their faces. This is very wrong, but I do believe that they had good intentions. They were just incapable of comprehending what a psychotic person goes through.

During this time, I was forced into the shower by three female staff who literally threw me onto the floor of the shower naked using excessive force. It was mean and humiliating, although I do understand that I needed a shower badly. I feel that they did not know how to properly approach the situation. I had the belief that I was going to be executed in the shower like the Jews were executed doing the Holocaust. I thought that electricity would come out of the showerhead along with the water. I was terrified to even think about taking a shower. I didn't want to die. It seemed that I couldn't try hard enough to survive. I thought I was bound and branded for death. There seemed to be no other alternative. After one month, when the insurance ran out, I was released from the hospital still psychotic.

March came and so did another psychiatric hospitalization. Just prior to the hospitalization I had accused my case manager of "trying to cut my neck with a knife", and her response was to call an ambulance. In my head, I honestly believed it to be truthful. In addition, my incest delusions and egg delusions became even stronger and more believable.

At this hospitalization, I striped off all my clothes, because the voices had ordered me to do so. I began believing that invisible doctors were taking over my mind and raping me in the butt and vagina. I thought these evil little microscopic doctors were invading my body and I had to kill them by pounding on my own body with my fists. I also believed they were raping me to turn me straight. They had apparently infested the whole hospital room and were collecting in my hair. I concluded that to remove them from my hair, I had to rip it out. So, that is what I did. I began to aggressively rip out huge amounts of my curly red hair, and I remember how painful it was.

Dr. Rodney's invisible being invaded my mind and began repeating the words "swinging in a tree". Also, I alleged that these invisible doctors were operating on my head and cutting out my brain, to turn me straight. They repeated in my mind the words "love and marriage." I was jumping around and hitting myself to try to remove these invaders.

Another delusion I had at the time was that the doctors had scientifically created life in the lab through the fusion of my eggs and Katie's eggs. Then I began to believe that they had given me invitro fertilization and impregnated me. They then removed the babies and grew them rapidly in a lab. I believed that they had removed the babies through C-section. And this was done six times, each producing two twin girls. I even remember that the first set of my twins were accidently cut through the "microscopic" C-section. One of the girl's hands had been accidently cut off and the other had been cut in the head.

Yet another delusion was the invisible rapes and the actual smell of sperm on my bed sheets, under my arms, and in my "fat folds". I believed these were the locations of my body that were being sexually assaulted. I even believed that the rapes had caused genital warts and that the doctors had burned them off when I was on the toilet seat. I had even seen a "genital wart scar" on me with my own two eyes. I also believed the invisible doctors were cutting into my labia and producing a flower shape. I was terrified to even use the toilet. After the genital warts and the mutilation, I felt that no one would ever want to love me, again.

I know now, looking back, that I was exceedingly insane. Being insane is a very difficult thing that most people cannot comprehend. It causes humongous amounts of fear, anxiety, and agony; and it leads to incredibly stupid behaviors.

Once again, after one month, the insurance ran out and I was released. After this hospitalization things began to fall apart even more. I contacted lawyers, newspapers, the police, and 911 with my stories about the medical researchers who were trying to kill me because I was gay. I told them about everything, including the "shocks" the perps were inflicting upon me. I needed someone desperately to help me, because I didn't want to die. I was terrified of death, and even just the thought of it. So, I began trying to reach out to others for help. I don't even know what really happens when you die. I guess you just cease to exist. You just stop thinking. You stop being. I did know, however, that whatever death was, I did not want to be any part of it!

At the end of March, while at my apartment, I began to believe that giant monsters from other planets, including the witches and a warlock, were invading my apartment and raping me. I believed that the police were fighting off these monsters in the parking lot of my apartment building.

I even recall believing that the world had ended. The new world had no need for bathrooms, as no one had any intestines or bladders anymore. When the sun went down that day, the world ended. When it came up, it was a completely different world. Somehow, I was slowly ridding the world of all evil. The evil people would come to try and find me, because they wanted to kill me. When they came for me, the police would kill them right outside my apartment building. Or so this is what I thought.

Chapter 17

KILLING THE WITCHES FOR GOD WITH FIRE

April 2015—May 16, 2015

As sure as April was to arrive, so were my delusions, and they seemed to be much more realistic. The radio continued to talk to me. The evil spirits were talking to me. The dead souls were talking to me. God was talking to me. I felt that God was using me in the most inhumane way, and His purpose was to rid the world of all evil. God had chosen me. I was the one. I was special. I was the second-coming of Christ. I was to be the savior by ridding the world of all its evil. Inside, I did not feel like I could do this, and I began to complain to God and He grew more and more angry with me. In other words, the voices became increasingly cruel and callous. I was at their mercy. I felt like there was nothing I could do, and that no one could help me now. I had tried to stop the perps, but there was nothing more I could do. God was communicating with me now. He wanted me to carry out His mission. I had no choice. I had to do something. Perhaps it was time for me to accept God's will.

That fateful night came on April 14th or 15th, I cannot recall exactly, at approximately 1:00am. It was a night just like all the nights had been for almost a year—darkness that was filled with intense fear and penetrating anxiety. I remember waking up instantly with a lighter in my hand, that I had fallen asleep with due to my addiction of three packs of cigarettes a day. God had ordered me with urgency, either through a dream, through a voice, or perhaps both, to start a fire to kill all the witches. He said He would kill me and I would burn in Hell for all of eternity if I refused. Filled with fear and impulsiveness I didn't even think twice. All I knew was that I didn't want to disobey God and suffer the consequence of going to Hell.

I don't think of myself as a bad person who would intentionally do anything like what I was about to do. In fact, I would consider myself a good person--a very good person with a heart of gold, who would do anything to help anyone in need. But I felt I was about to do this as an ultimate request from God to fulfill my legacy. And so, it happened.

After God gave me His imperative and crucial instructions to start a fire to kill all the witches. I did it. I mean I didn't want to go to Hell and burn in an eternal searing fire. So, because He had demanded that I did it instantly, I had no time to think. I just proceeded. I took the blue lighter, which was already in my hand, and lit a bunch of nearby dollar bills on fire. Then I put the burning bundle on the bed and attempted to start the sheets on fire. Then there was the call of nature, so I went to the bathroom. When I came back, I saw a huge fire. I was totally out of it at that point. I was criminally insane.

I ran out of the apartment almost naked. I was freaking out. There was heavy smoke everywhere and it was rising quickly. I was about to leave the apartment building when it came to me that I had to help my neighbors in the other apartments. I wanted to scream out to them but I was afraid of waking them up. I know that's weird. But anyways, I ran back into the burning bedroom, which was nearly engulfed in flames, and grabbed the cordless phone. I called 911 and told them that I had started a fire in my apartment, as I ran out of the burning building.

I stood outside for what seemed like the longest of times. I was wearing a short nightgown with nothing underneath. I recall I was cold, but mostly I was shocked and terrified by what had just happened. I thought I had done the right thing because God had told me to do it, but still my heart ached differently.

I watched the fire from the parking lot through my bedroom window. I watched the cops and two fire engines arrive. A male neighbor talked to me, and I recall telling him that I was now homeless and didn't know where I was going to live. I also remember fearing that I may have hurt someone, other than the witches. I told the cops the total truth when they questioned me, as the voices had always insisted that I be 100% honest all the time. And so, I was. I told them about the medical researchers in apartment eleven. I told them about the witches. I told them I had done it. I never spoke a lie, and to this day I am a big contender of always telling the truth and being totally honest no matter the consequences.

The cops read me my rights and placed me in their vehicle. I wasn't really understanding what was happening. I was totally out of it. Then they decided to place me in an ambulance, after strapping me to a stretcher. I was taken to the hospital once again. On the way there, I recall the ambulance hitting all the remaining witches and them turning to ashes which fell all over the ground and onto the windshield of the ambulance. During this time, I was extremely depressed and the most psychotic that I have ever been in my entire life. I kept on telling the workers at the hospital about the fire, because they'd ask. But I still thought it was what God wanted, and no one understood that. In fact, at the time, I felt like I was some sort of hero, because the witches were now dead, I had hoped, and I had put an end to the medical researchers' corrupt project.

The hospital stay was one-month long. During that time, I had no idea that I was in any sort of legal trouble. All I knew was that there had been a fire which I had started, I was homeless, and God wouldn't stop harassing me. I constructed all these spiritual concepts and ideas within my head. I was doing a video for each religion. The video was using only my voice, through my verbal shouts that were being recorded through microphones. But the videos would not have my body in them. I was told by the voices that I was too fat and ugly to be in their movies. Anyways, I had all these crazy religious thoughts. The movie I was making was called, "Holier than Thou" and that was me. I was the one who was the holiest. I constructed a case for the Episcopal religion, which was a religion I had been considering just prior to the fire. I was raised Catholic but had wanted to try a new religion.

Anyhow, a lot of the actual details of this hospital stay are scant in my memory. Perhaps I cannot recall them because of the amount of insanity that was in my head. All my thoughts were cloudy and rapidly racing from one topic to the next. My gullible and imaginative mind was being taken advantage of by my insanity, causing me to have unusual and ridiculous behaviors. I recall having the "vision" of being shot in the side by a cop. This area of my body was the place that my second soul had been. The first soul had been in my neck, and it had been removed due to a tumor. I believed that I was the only one who had two souls, and this was because I was the savior. Also during this hospitalization, I recall the medical researchers doing experiments on me, and giving me all artificial organs, including an alligator lung and pig intestines. The medical researchers also tried different permanent fragrances on me to alter the way my body smelled. As they tried each one on me, I could smell the scents changing. Some were pleasant, while others were putrid.

I was refusing to eat and shower. All I did was lie in bed all day at the hospital, like I had at home, and listened to God. He never shut up. The only relief I got was through sleep and that I tried to do a lot of. But no person can sleep all the time, even if they try. Maybe you can sleep all the time when you are dead, but I wasn't dead. I was surely alive, but what kind of life was I truly living. I had been living in fear for ten years, and I was now in serious trouble with the law, which I wasn't even capable of comprehending at that time.

I kept on having the delusion that God was raising up the hospital with all the dead souls, and taking me to heaven. I started having very specific detailed accounts of God, religion, and Heaven. I was now a "holy roller", as some people may call it. I had a deep connection with God and a deep understanding of spirituality, or so I thought. I was the only one special enough to be able to communicate directly with this higher power.

After a month stay at the hospital, I again was released due to insurance issues. This time two cops picked me up. I recall one of them giving me a big bottle of water. I didn't even understand what was really happening. I was still out of it, like I was in some other world. I thought that these cops were angels taking me to Heaven or demons taking me to Hell, because I thought I had died after being shot in the side.

As the cops sped off in their car, with me in the backseat, the scenery I saw through the window just seemed to go by too quickly, sort of like life. I remember believing that they had taken me into a different state. I still didn't even know I was in trouble at this point, and it would take many more months for me to realize this. Yep, 36 years old, and my life was over, but I didn't even know it. Perhaps, something would happen, a miracle possibly, that could change my fate. I guess I would just have to let things happen with time. What would be, would be.

Chapter 18

WHERE WAS I?

May 16, 2015—July 16, 2015

After arriving in this freakish place, I was put on a bench to wait for hours and hours. I was strip-searched and frisked. I remember having to bend over naked holding my butt cheeks open and cough. That was humiliating. I was not a criminal! My mind wasn't comprehending at all what was going on. I was mad. I was crazy. I was literally criminally insane!

I was there, but I did not know where there was. I believed it was Hell, but maybe it was somewhere else. I didn't know and the more I forced myself to try to figure it out, the crazier I got. I was so alone being the only one in my tiny cell and never being allowed out. There was a wooden platform to sleep on, and a rusty toilet, sink, and desk. It was quite a dirty and smelly place. I felt totally isolated, and I only saw someone when they brought my meals, but they never talked to me. Sometimes they even forgot to feed me. Only about five times in those two months in that dark dungeon, was I forced to take a shower. I was out of it. Too out of it and too afraid to really be embarrassed to be watched taking a shower.

I feared that I could be murdered at any time, and it didn't help that a cop threatened to pepper spray me if I didn't stop screaming. I began to radically accept the fact that I was going to die. I consulted with God constantly through prayer. At least I could talk to Him, because there was no one in this dungeon that would listen to me.

I did nothing but lie there on that filthy wooden platform naked, and mope around with my delusional thoughts. The green garb I was placed in for nearly the entire two months was extremely uncomfortable so I refused to wear it. I had been placed in garb because I was considered a threat to myself and others. It wasn't until months later that I understood where I had been. I had been in solitary confinement for almost two months. I was in a jail!

It was so hard for me to comprehend how someone like myself could be in such a horrible place as jail. I had always been a respectable and law-abiding citizen. My being in jail was hard for me, and those who knew me, to believe. Still it was very valid reality.

My psychosis did not clear up in jail. In fact, it only became much more severe. I was constantly living in fear. I continued having intense delusions and hallucinations. My mind

177

was spinning further and further out of control and I felt helpless, not to mention hopeless that I would even survive. I felt that no one could help me, not even a psychiatrist. Sure, they asked me if I was hearing voices but I would always tell them that I wasn't. I, myself, couldn't understand what was truly going on within my own brain.

My delusions varied greatly and included themes from sexual content to religious and governmental topics. There was also the nagging delusion about the witches. My thoughts were quite ridiculous, and they led to many unreasonable behaviors, while I was spending my time rotting away in jail. I screamed loudly, repeatedly, the entire time I was there, and refused to cooperate with the prison officials, because I feared them. I was very worried that I wouldn't survive, and I was very loud and erratic as I continued to protest the voices.

At first, I thought I was being locked up as part of a "soulmate project". The medical researchers were finally going to pay me back for ruining my life by giving me a new lover in my life. Each time I saw someone, which was rarely, I thought that this person had been chosen to be my perfect match. I was falling in love with almost every female that I saw from cops to inmates.

Then I thought I was in this place to study to become a doctor or a psychologist. I was answering my voices' questions quite accurately and I passed all the tests that the voices had given to me. I believed that I was now a real doctor. Then I passed the exams to become a psychologist. I only had to make a choice between the two occupations. I believe I had these delusions because of my intense desire to become a doctor or psychologist, which had not been fulfilled, causing extreme regrets in my subconscious mind.

I came up with a military setup as well. I thought I was training for the army or doing some sort of government project. Regarding government, I believed that the president had and was now raping me for a video. I thought he was using me as a sex slave. It didn't help that he was invisible to me, just like all the other evil entities that were attacking me.

Then there was the belief that I had died in the fire and that I was on God's workbench. He was reconstructing me from the ashes so He could reincarnate me into a new life. I believed I was the reincarnation of Jesus Christ, Joan of Arc, and many other heroic figures. I assumed that several of the people I knew had come to rescue me and had been taken captive and put in other cells. I thought I was in some sort of church or spiritual building in which I was being forced to choose the correct religion or be punished with the loss of my life. I believed they were going to burn me alive in the cremation center, which I alleged was in another area of this building that held me prisoner. I began talking to God and to the Devil. I didn't know who was who. Somehow everything was inverted and flipped around in my mind. I knew I had to choose the good entity over the evil one, or I would be punished by God for all of eternity. I even constructed a story in my head about "God the Father".

I was hearing music on a constant basis, which I believed was supposed to alter my thoughts through subliminal messages. I thought that the "evil Satan worshippers" where dissecting my body and creating a machine out of me. I thought that university students were giving me an artificial brain and doing "cranial mastectomies" on me by sawing off pieces of my skull and rearranging the "neurotransmitters" in my brain to transform me into a new human being. I believed they were trying to fix my "homosexual problem", which was rooted in my deepest and most "innate" neurotransmitters. They told me that when they pulled the "cord" in the back of my brain, it would cause me to go blind. Then my skull would shatter into a million pieces and all the neurotransmitters would fall out. Then they could modify each neurotransmitter and put them back together in any way they chose. This was done to reconstruct me into a new human being with new characteristics, personality, and experiences.

I felt I had extraordinary capabilities, such as psychic and telekinetic powers. I was the only living human being with all "five gifts", including foresight, the gift of having "visions", and a winking ability that allowed me to communicate secretly with people. I had been given a bad gift though which my voices called "hindsight." My "gifts" were installed in the back of my skull in my neurotransmitter chips. I remember accusing an inmate, who was helping me in the shower, of stealing my "motor chips". These "chips" controlled the ability to walk, and I was having difficulty doing even that because it felt like my knee caps were detaching. The truth being was that I was having much difficulty doing almost everything.

My psychic powers were allowing me to scream out bank account numbers of people I didn't know. They also allowed me to solve crimes and identify the location and type of crime that was being committed at the exact time it was happening. I then believed I was in a "cop hangout" to help the cops do this. The police could hear things through the "radio transmitter" that was placed in my back ten years earlier. I thought they were protecting me from my family, who I believed was extremely evil. Also, at one time, I believed that the cops had taken me hostage to use me to make porn videos.

I began believing my family was trying to kill me with the lights that were installed in my cell. They were electrocuting me and "cooking" me through these lights. I assumed they had this ability because my brother's skills in electrical engineering. Their motive, like so many other times, was simply because I was gay. I began to recreate a family tree in my mind. I thought that my family had murdered my Aunt Betty, and began to believe that this place I was in, was serving her dead body parts ground up on the food trays. The voices disclosed to me that if I ate everything on the tray, I would die a terrible death like my aunt had. I tasted mashed potatoes made from an old rubber sole of a cop boot.

I then began to connect all the pieces and all the generations. I was a descendent of Adolf Hitler, and that is why, I assumed, my brother Roger had a fascination with the man and was creating a holocaust for the homosexual population. Then I considered that the members of my family were dead and that evil spirits had taken over their bodies.

Then there was the "witch hunt". I could call on all the witches through my telekinetic powers. They would come to this place to attack me, but before they could get to me the cops would execute them. I even heard the guns going off! I had the capacity to send the witches to Hell through my verbalizations. I believed that Hell was in the sewers of the building that I now resided in. I heard the voices of the witches from the drains and I made every attempt to stop them from coming back up the pipes from Hell. The voices even insisted that I shit in the drain to feed the witches in Hell.

Hearing guns and evil music were only two of the many auditory hallucinations that I was having. Every idea that the voices gave to me became an ingrained delusion. Besides hearing things, my psychosis was also affecting my other four senses. I began seeing things such as myself as a child in the little mirror above the corroded sink. I was just a little child of four or five years old. That was freaky, but I continued to stare at my younger self and I couldn't believe what I was seeing with my own two eyes. I also saw my body transforming from fat to skinny in just a matter of seconds. I saw the cops dressed like fairies, and

I believed that they were shocking me repeatedly in the head with stun guns. My head just didn't feel right at all. I also saw an inmate flaunting in front of my little cell window on the door, trying to seduce me with her "big hair". That one is kind of hard to explain.

I was smelling odors including sweat, sperm, and vaginal fluid, which really weren't there. I was tasting sperm and vaginal fluid. I felt myself being choked and I did vomit. It landed all over my food tray. I was feeling myself getting "plucked out", as the voices called it, and raped. The evil spirits were raping me through my blanket, which the voices caused a "fish net". They were requiring me to have sex with a man and marry him to end my homosexuality. The man who gave me the first orgasm was the one I was required to marry.

I remember thinking that invisible doctors were working on me. One of the things they did was reconstruct my vagina because all the rapes I had endured had destroyed it. I believed that I had contracted every sexually transmitted disease that existed from the rapes of the spirits and the cops, who were making videos of the assaults to sell on the internet. The delusion that I had STDs was only reinforced when I saw and felt genital warts on myself in the shower. That frightened me very much when I felt them, not only in my private area, but also all over my thighs. Also, I had the delusion that the government was invisibly removing clits and switching them in women. I thought I gotten stung by a bee there and that the government had lasered holes in my clit.

The insanity would continue. I believed that I was being monitored by cameras, even ones under the toilet seat. And I was being recorded by skype that was installed in the walls of my cell, giving access to the entire world. I thought Hollywood was involved. I thought I was famous, but then concluded that I was only being used to make these videos for free. I was the mind and voice behind Heidi and many other movies. I had written the story of Heidi when I was a kid, and I was her voice in the movie. My mom had taken my compensation from that.

I began believing that I was "God's only daughter", and that I had the ability to end the world at any time. I began screaming out "end the world". At one point, I thought I had really ended it. The whole world had died, and I was now alone and would eventually die too, from starvation.

I remember believing that the cops had found the picture of Jesus I had thrown away, in a landfill. They were passing this powerful and vandalized picture among them. I thought that by staring into the sun behind Jesus's head that you could change from Christian to Atheist and back if you wanted to. I thought that since I was the holiest one, if I stared deeply into someone eyes, I could change them from being an evil person into a good one. I began to try this on cops, social workers, and inmates on the few occasions that I saw someone. But it didn't seem to be working because these "people" still had me locked in this "room". I was desperately longing to be free, and my delusions were giving me the hope that I would be leaving soon. They only turned around and disappointed me.

Once a nice officer brought me some books. I recall I had asked her for a Bible, but she said she didn't have one of those. I began seeing different words than were actually printed on the pages of the book. Not just different words but whole different sentences and paragraphs. I had written a new "holy book" with the power of my mind. This experience was like the two books I had recreated in my mind before I was incarcerated.

Also, I can remember believing that I was a student in an aeronautical engineering program. I thought that I was on a rocket ship and was being taken to different planets. The inmates who brought my food were aliens from different planets.

I remember believing that the different cops I saw were zombies whose bodies had been taken over by the evil members of my family. I began to believe that my family members were the people who were holding me hostage, and that this place was actually a room in my grandfather's bomb shelter.

I remember the voices telling me to flush toilet repeatedly, and I listened to them. The voices claimed that flushing the toilet signified the end of the project and I wanted that so badly. So, I just stood there and flushed it repeatedly. I also remember eating hair and bugs that had fallen onto my food trays and into my water cups. I was told that I had to eat the bugs to kill the evil spirits. I had my period twice but did nothing about it. I just laid there in blood and assumed that I had a cyst that had broken. I also had the belief that the invisible people had shaved my pubic hair for their porn videos of me.

There were delusions about Egyptians who were gypsies. There was the belief that I was a healer, and I could heal my own body from the electricity's effects with the words "heal my body", as I swished my hand through the air over the length of my entire body. And it appeared to work. I felt healed at that moment.

Also, I believed the delusion that I was forming caves below the jail, through my screaming which was like a stick of dynamite. They told me they were paying me to do this, because there was a lot of hidden gold involved. So, I just kept yelling at the top of my lungs.

Every time they came into my cell to give me a shot of Ativan, I believed that I was receiving the lethal injection. The shot would kill me in twenty minutes and I counted away the minutes until I would be dead. I believed that the invisible beings were giving me "heroin and cocaine patches" to mess with my brain chemistry. Also, I thought that these evil, invisible things were going up my butt and into my intestines and getting caught there. I thought I had to shit them all out while trying not to get any of them caught in my anal hairs. Also, going on in my mind was the thought that I was being treated for brain cancer, through the walls with this experimental electrical system that was designed to shrink the tumors.

I thought the medical researchers, who looked like big hairy monsters with mean voices, had continued their project in this new place that I was at. I believed they were taking my intestines out through my anus and clearing the blockages out and then putting them back inside me. I felt them putting their fingers into my anus, causing the gas to be released and bowel movements to occur. I also thought that my real mother was a medical researcher from England, and she was coming by plane to take me home.

I thought that I was in a different realm, because I had ended the world above by command. I was instructed to do this because the outer world were not Christians and now all the Christians had to live underground in this prison, because the upper world was on fire. We were running out of food, so one of the Christians would have to go into the outer world and try to find some food. Now that I had ended the world, we had no choice but to live in this underground dungeon.

At one time, I thought I was in some sort of church or "evil Satan worshipping house". They were trying to get me to become one of them through their continuous verbal threats in my head. There were different levels of the Church— one was the holding cell, one was the solitary confinement cell, and one was the medical cell. I recall killing two bugs when I was in the "Pentecostal Church", and I was reprimanded by the voices for murdering the insects.

Ok. Well that was that. Being there in that jail was an experience I will never forget and one that I never want to go through again. My mind just raced with delusional thoughts that brought terror into my already scarred life. The hallucinations only increased and reinforced my delusions, and therefore my fear became amplified as well.

I was finally committed to the Center of Forensic Psychiatry after two full months in jail. I was determined by a psychiatrist to be mentally incompetent to stand trial. I was relieved to some degree, because this hospital seemed to be a little better of a place than jail had been. I did not know what would happen there. I did not know if I would continue to live a life filled with the fear of being killed, or if somehow, I could get past this disabling fear.

Chapter 19

BEING INVOLUNTARILY COMMITTED

July 16, 2015—January 2016

On July 16th, 2015, I was committed to the Center of Forensic Psychiatry (CFP) which is intended for people who had committed crimes while they were insane. Half the people there were deemed incompetent to stand trial (IST) and the other half were there after receiving the not guilty by reason of insanity (NGRI) decision. I remember believing that I was the only "special one" there. I wasn't there as an IST or NGRI. I was there for protection only, and the voices in my head just confirmed this.

I would be there as both an IST and NGRI for a period totaling 16 months. It was there that my delusions and hallucinations would continue for the next several months, until I was finally stabilized on the correct medications.

I was taken there by a court vehicle—a big truck-like vehicle with two giant locked cages on it. I remember the female inmates, that were being transported with me, were being perverted with the male inmates in the other locked compartment through the window that was between the two cages. These inmates seemed rough and tough, and I knew that I wasn't one of them. I was so sweet and innocent. I never, ever, would have imagined myself in a situation like this one in my entire life. Somehow my life had fallen apart, but at the time, I was too sick to understand why.

When being admitted, I thought I was working for the FBI and that this new place was my next setting where I would help the federal government, because I was finished helping the cops. I felt I was special and could help them by using my psychic abilities, which I still felt I had.

When they took my booking photo, I thought it was just a photo for my new job ID. And then they weighed me. I didn't comprehend at all what was truly going on. I felt like I was in my own world, while the outside world just continued to spin out of control. But, in fact, it wasn't the outside world that was losing control. It was the inside world—my brain.

I began to believe I was being locked in this terrible place to protect me from my "evil family". They were trying to kill me, and this was determined to be the safest place for me while the police investigated. My family was guilty of many crimes, including, but not limited to, murder, rape, and money laundering. I believed that I had suffered incest as a child and that I had given birth to children who had been given to my cousins and brothers to raise. I also believed my family had murdered some of the children I bore when they were just newborns. I thought they had been buried in my parents' backyard. I believed the rapes had occurred at nighttime when they injected me with some sort of drug to knock me out. I also believed that my mother had given me huge amounts of aspirin to cause me to miscarry some of the babies.

Here is a recorded inscription I wrote in my notebook during my stay at the CFP. It is quoted exactly word for word: "My family are 'incesters'. They raped me over and over. They killed 8 children of mine. They stole my eggs. They raped me at their house, my two apartments, and at their bomb shelter (constructed by my grandfather at his old residence). Their friends were involved. They hired people to try to turn me straight. They killed my wife and her son. They used drugs on me to put me asleep to rape me. They put porn of me on internet and stole my internet businesses. They were sexually, physically, emotionally, mentally, and financially abusive. My mom's family members also raped me. Michelle and Roger killed Betty. Michelle killed 500 people at the hospital in the recovery room. I was Heidi. They stole the money. They stole my inheritance from Betty, my real mom. Everyone at that jail raped me. They fried my head at the jail through electroconvulsive rays and tricyclics. At my apartment, Roger struck me in the head with electricity through the electrical sockets. I had a child here at Forensics. Victor is the father. I had 5 kids at Tulip Valley. They killed them. I had triplets at my apartment. Victor killed them . . . Roger is the head of the Mafia. The NSA are involved."

In addition, recorded in the notebook was: "My whole family is guilty! They stole all my babies!!! Fuck off!! I am taking them ALL back." Also noted was ". . . I have 539 children from the eggs they stole from me as a teenager. 554 total kids." God said through a voice I could audibly hear, "They (my family) killed so many people it's pathetic. They killed more than 41." And so, I refused to call anyone in my family, or even talk to them when they called me on the patient telephone. After a few months, I did answer one of their calls, but still felt deep down inside that they were extremely evil people, even though that may have been far from the truth. That was pure insanity, but that was only just the beginning.

I began believing that the male doctors at the hospital were raping me for a project, that was led by psychiatrists, to change my sexual orientation. Reported in my notebook was: "The male doctors are raping me as invisible men. I hate them."

Noted, in addition, was: "They are using magnetic radio on me." I had the delusion that magnetic radio was how I was hearing these things. It was being used in conjunction with the radio transmitter that I believe the doctors had installed in my back.

I remember feeling that I was "communicating with live souls." I had the ability to hear what other people were thinking in their minds. I was connecting with the innermost part of their souls. I positively knew what the other patients and the staff were thinking. I heard it in my mind through the voices that continued to plague me.

Suddenly, I was hearing God's voice again. He was reinforcing that I was indeed the Second-Coming of Christ. Inscribed in my notebook was this: "This was a battle between God and the devil. And now the devil is dead. I AM CHRIST."

God was telling me that I could produce miracles like Jesus Christ had. He ordered me to complete the "natural cures project". He was giving me the cures naturally of many different diseases, some cancers, into which natural cures were not known. I noted everything God told me in a notebook, using a marker. This project would be worth billions, and I was instructed to give the money I made from it to charity.

I recall that grass was the cure for bad eyesight, including total blindness. So, I tested it for myself. I began eating grass, on a rare occasion that we were allowed outside in a closed-in-area secured with electrical fences. Despite my belief that it would work, it didn't. My vision was not improving and I couldn't understand why God's cure wasn't working on me. I just assumed that God was not offering me this cure for myself because I was "the special one", and I was the exception. It is noted in my journal that "Boron is the miracle element", which meant that it was the cure for many diseases, including many types of cancer. Also written, among much, is that the cure for chronic fatigue syndrome is to eat lots of animal fat; that a natural pain-relieving agent is consumption of moss; and that the cure for Alzheimer's disease is flax seed.

God told me He was going to grant each "good" human being a wish. They could have anything that they wanted. The "live souls" of the staff and patients began to communicate with me. Some men chose to have bigger muscles, and one even chose a bigger penis to satisfy his wife.

Some women chose to have bigger breasts or to become pregnant. They could even choose how many months they wanted to be along. Instantly, the wishes were granted. Muscles, penises, and breasts became larger. I saw it happen with my own eyes. And suddenly, non-pregnant women conceived immaculately. There were even pregnant virgins now! And my visual hallucinations only verified this.

God then commanded me to write a new Bible, and began telling me what to compose on the paper. He instructed me about everything from it being ok to be gay, to being ok to have one romantic tattoo and to being ok to have a drink occasionally. He said, "NEVER say I love everyone, ever again!" I was directed by God's voice telling me that I would be the author of this "new Bible" that was intended to replace the original one. He also coached me that as the new Christ, I would be responsible for changing the entire world and making it a good place to live in again.

Some of the things God told me were: "This whole thing has gone too far. Now I am causing storms all over . . . now we are going to have a flood everywhere . . . Soon there will be no Earth, because I am pissed . . . You will go to Heaven . . . Everyone else is going to Hell . . . And they cannot pray to change it . . . You will die at 5 o'clock exactly . . . you will die by drowning. It is the worst form of death . . . And Stephanie, I am sorry you worked so hard, but now the world must end. They won't like Hell, because it is dark, freaky, spooky, insane, and everybody shoots at each other and then they become dead again and go to Nothingness."

The people on the television began having conversations with me as well, especially the news programs. I even recall being able to tell when someone had had good sex the night before and the reporters telling me to please stop telling the world about their sex lives.

God began talking to me again, only to my surprise was that God was now my aunt Betty. The old God had retired and she was chosen to become the new God. She was talking to me and I recall her telling me how much she missed and loved me. She also told me that she was my real mother and that I was really Christ. It felt good to finally have the ability to talk to her again after losing her over ten years earlier.

After a few months, I pondered my life and tried to figure out what would make me happy, because truly there was no bit of happiness left within me, having to deal with the constant fear of God's voice. I thought getting Katie back would make me happy, but she returned the letter I had written her. On the unopened envelope, she wrote that if I contacted her again she would get a restraining order against me. Feeling defeated, I told myself I was in love with my former case manager and I sent her five letters which she later returned to me. I wanted love so bad. Anyone to love would be fine. I remembered that when I had Katie's love it was the best and happiest time of my entire life.

I wrote my new love, whomever she would be, a proposal. As recorded:

"My Dearest, today is the greatest day of my entire life. Today I vow to you great happiness, undying faithfulness, and romantic love. It is this commitment that comes from my own heart. I want to hold your hand tenderly, kiss your body, and make passionate love to you. But mostly, I want to know your heart and soul. You really are such a beautiful woman inside and out. I know we have a lifetime together and I do love you. And I want us to be together through all times— good and bad. I will always be there for you until the day I die. I want you to know I'll never judge you or hurt you in any way. I want to take this incredible life journey with you, because I love you. And God loves you so much that He is giving me to you right now." Then God said there was to be a kiss.

I even wrote several love poems in my notebook including this one:

"Love. A love so true. There has never been a love, as deep as you."

Despite my endless longing to have love in my life again, I sadly realized that there would be none. Katie didn't want me back and my case manager thought I was crazy. Anyways, no one would want a crazy bitch with so much baggage and such a bad past. I was getting tired and sick of being locked up in this hospital. I felt trapped and this can be seen with this statement found in my notebook, "I want out of this fuckin' place. This is a hate crime." I became hopeless and felt lost and terribly alone. This only led me to have more suicidal thoughts. I have this angry poem about death, that was recorded in my notebook:

"Death. To die is all I want to do. Yes, it's true. Fuck this place. All I want to do is escape. Fuck these people! Fuck life! Fuck Katie! Fuck my family! Fuck all! Fuck everything! Fuck YOU!"

Also found in the journal was a suicide note. It was the belief that if I killed myself that the entire world would end as well, because that is what God had told me. The note read:

"Now is the correct time. I have no choice now. All you mother fuckers care about is stealing my money and using me. This world sucks. Good-bye world. Good-bye. Suicide is the only answer. And everyone knows it. They are all guilty. They are all going to burn in Hell. The world is ending tonight at midnight. Just 11 hours left of this shitty life. At least I'm going to Heaven and I am the only one. So, fuck the world. Fuck life. I am going to Heaven to be with my mom. I just can't do this anymore. Life sucks. I have nothing and no one. I give up. Fuck everything and everyone. Fuck you! Fuck you all. I can't believe they are doing this to me. Now suicide is mine. I own suicide. I WANT KATIE BACK NOW!!!!"

The last sentence of that note reflected that unless Katie came back into my life, I would commit suicide which would thus lead to the end of the world as we know it.

Of course, as you can see since I'm writing this, I never succeeded at committing suicide. There probably would have been no way with all the security measures they had at that state mental hospital. I thought I could rip the carotid artery out of my neck and die that way, but I knew it would be too hard to accomplish. I wondered what I should do next. I was locked in this terrible place with crazies and criminals, and there seemed to be no way out. There were no answers to solve all the many problems I had. I just didn't know what to do to correct all the wrongs that my life contained, but I did know that I had to try something and do it fast.

Chapter 20

BEGINNING MY RECOVERY

February 2016—November 11, 2016

I finally made the decision to try to ignore the voices, instead of letting them "entertain" me. I got a headphone radio to help I drown out the disturbing voices. Also, they stabilized me on three psychiatric medications—one for depression, one for mood swings, and one for psychosis. Gradually, I noticed less intensity in the voices. They were slowly fading away. Thanks be to God. But now I began feeling even more alone. As the voices began to disappear, so did their company. Sure, it was bad company, but at least it was some sort of comradeship.

I now had only myself to rely upon. I knew that I had to find inner love to get me through my horrible incarceration. It would be a difficult task, because I couldn't figure out how anyone, who had been through all that I had, could love themselves. I was crazy and I had to come to the realization that I was truly mentally sick. I did have schizoaffective disorder, and I needed to take medications for the rest of my life. I had to allow myself to radically accept that. I felt that I had no other choice. If I couldn't kill myself, I had to figure out some way to survive.

I began telling myself that these were only voices in my head. They were not actual people talking to and about me. They were caused by a chemical imbalance within my brain. I was not at fault in any way. I had an illness that required continual treatment.

It also was very helpful to engage in what I called "self-therapy". During this process, I had to correct each delusion that I had believed was reality. This was very draining, time consuming, and mentally exhausting. But I slowly began to accept that each of the many delusions I had were in fact just that—delusions. After disregarding every delusion, I had to reconstruct and accept the truth in my life. I had to establish the facts of who I was, where I had been, and were I intended on going. It was a slow process that seemed to drag on forever.

I was me, but who was me? I was a smart and talented woman who had been inflicted with a severe mental illness. But despite that, I was a very kind person. I had helped many people in my life. I valued friendship and family. I was just your overall good person who happened, perhaps by fate, to have a devastating mental illness.

My past had been a wild roller coaster ride, but I choose not to let my past define me. I will not let myself be a victim. I will be a survivor.

My future was open to anything. I just wanted to be happy again one day and I had to force myself to believe that this would happen. I had to know in my heart that I would find true happiness again in the future.

With the medications, the headphone radio, and the "self-therapy", I got rid of the voices all together. I had been inflicted with voices on and off for nearly thirteen years. But now I was freed from them after over two consecutive years of them holding me hostage!

After being in the hospital for almost seven months, I was evaluated and deemed competent to stand trial. I was taken back to jail in February but there had been a mistake, so they returned me to the CFP. In March, I spent another long week in jail, awaiting my trial, but it was postponed due to the wintery weather. I clearly remember spending my 37th birthday behind bars with a "bunkie" who was a bank robber. Being in jail during my birthday was tough, and I remember I cried a lot during that time.

In April, I stood trial after again being returned to jail. The judge's decision was that I should be committed to CFP for further observation and treatment. I was given the status of "Not Guilty by Reason of Insanity", which had been altered from the previous one of "Incompetent to Stand Trial". After being handed down the decision, I felt obligated to apologize for what I had done while I was insane. And I did tell the judge that I was truly sorry.

Time seemed to move by ever so slowly while I was at the CFP, but my life did seem to be moving in a positive upward direction. I could have been sentenced to 20 years in prison with tough criminals as my only companions. However long I had to be in this hospital, I knew that it was better than being incarcerated in a prison. I had to find positive things to keep myself going. I had to force myself to smile, even though I felt that there was no reason to do so. At least I was alive and my mental illness was being treated. Under no circumstance would I ever want to go through this again. Jail was *horrible*, but at least the hospital was just *bad*.

Over the next several months, I started to routinely pray to God. I begged Him to deliver me from this Hell that I was in. My voices had vanished and I was no longer a harm to myself or others. I was stable mentally but I continued to remain at the CFP where an exciting day was going to the vending machines, which was a privilege up to two times a week. I thought sipping water from a drinking fountain was also a real treat. I had no freedom. I couldn't go out to a movie or dinner. I couldn't even take a walk down the street to get some fresh air. I willed that God would help me. This whole thing was not my fault. I had been very, very, sick. But I was feeling a lot better now, and I desired to move forward with my life.

I was told all the facts. I would have to be on a five-year contract when I was released from the CFP, in which I could not leave my state without permission. In the contract, they could restrict whatever they wanted in my case, but at least I wouldn't have a record as a convicted felon. I had to try to see all the positives in my situation.

I continued my days there at the CFP in a daze, like a fog that wouldn't lift. I was bored, tired, and a bit depressed. I knew that the only one that could help me now, was God. He would help me, and I that is what I chose to believe. I prayed and prayed until my day of true deliverance finally arrived.

I had a court hearing the end of October 2016 to review my case. My psychiatrist testified that I was not a harm to myself or others. So, the judge had no choice but to do the right thing. I was to be released from the CFP, and I would be freed without any contract being in place! This was never heard of in the long history of the CFP. Again, I had been the exception to the rule. I would now be free to live my life however I wanted. I could go anywhere, live anywhere, and do whatever I wanted with my life. I had been given my freedom and my life back. It was truly a miracle, and I believe that it was God who had done this for me.

As my release date of November 11th, 2016 closed in, I was getting very nervous. I had been locked up for so long, I feared having the responsibilities of an adult. I understood that I would have obligations to fulfill, but I also knew that I would be free to do whatever I wanted in life. I longed to get an apartment and a car again someday. I wanted to write a memoir, this one in fact, and I longed to make it a best seller. Then after the publishing of the book, I hoped to go into mental health freelance writing and possibly become a peer support specialist.

I knew I had been given a second chance at life. This was truly a gift from God Himself. I knew I would never take anything for granted ever again. Because no matter how hard I thought life was back in my past, it was never as bad as being incarcerated for a total of eighteen months. To this day, I thank God, every free moment I have for my freedom and for my very life. I have been truly blessed.

Chapter 21

GETTING MY FREEDOM BACK

November 11, 2016—May 2017

On November 11th, 2016, I was released from the CFP and sent to a crisis center. I had been unable to find a place to live with such short notice and the CFP had been forced to abide with the release date that the court had stated. My mother wanted to put me in a group home, but I had different plans. Since there was no contract in place, I wanted to obtain an apartment, but no one was willing to help me.

After an unproductive week in this crisis center, I was told that I would be released to a homeless shelter the very next day. I was scared and didn't know what to do. All I knew was that I did not want to be homeless, and I feared that homelessness would cause my impending death. The mere thought of that, scared the living shit out of me.

Not knowing what else to do, I called my mother, crying, and reported my devastating situation to her. She was very reluctant to help me find an apartment. What she wanted was to find me "a nice group home", and she did try but there were no openings available in group homes for the next day. She didn't want me to be homeless either, and thank God, she cared. She eventually gave in and agreed to help me find an apartment and move in, but only if I complied with her wishes. She wanted me to move back to my hometown, where she still lived.

Wow! The first the miracle was not going to prison for a very long time. Then there was the miracle of being released without restrictions. And now the miracle of getting a new place, that wasn't a group home, to live with a fresh, new start. God was certainly looking out for me. I was happier and more thankful then I had been in a very long time. This was perhaps the most contented and most grateful time in my entire life.

And so, I was moving forward in life, but I knew that there would be many challenges and obstacles along the way. There always are. I had lost the entirety of my belongings in the fire and I needed everything for my new apartment. My family supplied me with many second-hand items, which I was truly glad to receive. I didn't need new things, and anyways, I couldn't afford all first-hand items. I even picked up some furniture from a thrift store down the street from where I lived.

After getting myself settled into my new apartment, I had the task of trying to get my medical insurance and disability benefits back intact. This proved to be a very difficult task, because everything was either suspended or revoked when I was in the hospital. Many visits and calls to the local Social Security office and nearby Department of Human Services were involved. But I knew that this, too, would eventually work out.

I got my old primary doctor back. I also reapplied for mental health services from the place I had gone as a teenager. They set me up with a new psychiatrist who prescribed me my psych meds. He issued me the same meds I had been given in the hospital. I knew I had to continue taking these meds for life, if I wanted to remain stable and out of trouble. That is what I wanted and needed to be.

Since I didn't have a car, I relied on rides from family, friends, and a transportation service. Quickly after returning to my home town, I reunited with two old friends, one whom I met in high school and the other, Joshua, a guy who I met when I was 21 years old. They were very supportive in my efforts to improve my life, and they brought many bright and beautiful days to me. Not to mention that my supportive family also helped me to a very large degree.

As for my mental stability, it was there. And I knew it would remain there, since I was taking my pills continually, as prescribed, at the correct times. Also, I began walking for exercise, eating right, and getting the appropriate amount of sleep each night. Getting enough sleep is very important. The number one rule for myself was that I must abstain from excessive stress and not push myself too hard.

I began having high hopes for the future. I established goals—getting a car, writing this memoir and having it become a best seller, becoming a peer support specialist, and doing mental health freelance writing. Sure, it's not as prestigious as my goal of becoming a doctor, but it was something. I knew I had to let go of my hope of ever becoming a doctor, because it wasn't my fate. God had a different purpose for my life. And I believed that my new dreams could perhaps be that purpose.

Speaking of God, I wanted to continue to have His blessings in my life. So, I prayed daily and thanked him for my life and for my freedom, which was something I rarely had done in the past. God was truly there, with me, looking out for my welfare, and it was time to praise Him for His help and for all the good things that I did have in life—my family, my friends, and my freedom. If I really think hard, I am sure the list of things to be grateful for would go on and on.

Sure, my life had been a living Hell, where nothing seemed to go right. My mental illness had exhausted the happiness out of every fiber of my being, and had created a constant state of fear. The disease that I had been inflicted with had ruined my dreams, my hopes, my goals. But certainly, God allowed me to go through what I had, because He had His dreams, hopes, and goals for my life. I had to accept that His will shall be done, not my own selfish plans for my life.

I will continue to move forward and pursue a life of goodness, love, and prosperity; but will only do so if God wills it.

AUTHOR'S NOTE TO YOU:

Dear Reader,

Thank you for reading this book!

If you liked this memoir, please feel free to comment on it with a review. Also, it would be very much appreciated if you would recommend this book to others who you feel could benefit from it in any way. This is an effort to spread the awareness of mental illness and stop all the stigma associated with it.

I can be contacted, for any reason, at StephanieAllen1979@gmail.com. I will respond to each email as promptly as possible.

I sincerely hope you have much joy and love in your life.

With Loving Regards,

Stephanie

Made in the USA
San Bernardino, CA
09 January 2020

62920790R00132